Mentors Matter but Poverty Sucks

By

Eugene L. Moore, Ph.D.

Mentors Matter But Poverty Sucks
By Eugene L. Moore, Copyright 2018

ISBN: 978-1-947288-33-1

All rights reserved solely by the author. Except where designated, the author certifies that all contents are original and do not infringe upon the legal rights of any other person. No part of this book may be reproduced in any form without permission in writing from the publisher, except in the case of brief quotations embodied in critical articles or reviews.

10 9 8 7 6 5 4 3 2 1

Printed in the United States of America

Cover design by: Treviante Brown

Published by: Life To Legacy, LLC

P.O. Box 1239

Matteson, IL 60443

877-267-7477

www.Life2Legacy.com

TABLE OF CONTENTS

Editor's Notes 4

About the Author 5

Dedication 7

Acknowledgments 8

Foreword 13

Author's Message of Hope 15

Preface 19

Chapter 1 Introduction to the Research 20

Chapter 2 Literature Review 32

Chapter 3 Methodological Approach and Research Design 53

Chapter 4 Research Findings 73

Chapter 5 Discussion of Findings 126

Chapter 6 Discussion, Implications and Conclusion 148

Closing Remarks On the Run 158

References 160

Appendix A Youth Participant Interview Questions 178

Appendix B Youth Participant profiles 180

Appendix C Staff Participant Interview Questions 181

Eugene L. Moore, Ph.D.

Editor's Notes

The editor and Dr. Moore are neighbors and close friends. Our backgrounds are very far afield making for some bazaar conversations and lively debate. In December 1959, my dad received a major promotion with a paper company and our family moved from Portland, Oregon to Bogalusa, Louisiana. I was almost ten. Before we moved, I quite literally had never even seen a black person. I expected everyone to look like Aunt Jemima and work in cotton fields.

I almost fell off my chair, when I watched Walter Cronkite's year-in-review-1965 CBS broadcast — Bogalusa had made the top ten national news stories. Quick research reveals these news titles and more: *Bogalusa, Louisiana* — *"Klantown USA"*, *CORE Comes to Bogalusa*, *CORE and the Deacons Confront the Klan*, *The Klan Strikes Back*, and *Bloody Bogalusa*. Our neighbors directly across the street had a cross burned in their front yard.

Dr. King was assassinated on my 18th birthday. I was a senior and Bogalusa schools had just integrated that year. There were no African-American seniors and only thirteen in the junior class. At graduation in a traditional ceremony honoring academics, the top ten female seniors walked in procession with the top ten juniors, carrying an ivy chain between them. I changed places with another girl whose rank placed her next to a black scholar — her father forbade her to walk next to a black girl, even one with high-academic achievement.

The lived experiences of African-American at-risk teens are the backdrop of this book. But Dr. Moore acknowledges poverty as a colorblind problem. He *speaks truth to power* confronting those who hold important positions and demanding a moral response to the problem of poverty.

Brenda Husler

ABOUT THE AUTHOR

It has been just over a year since Eugene L. Moore, Ph.D. published the final book of his trilogy titled *Still Learning and Still Tweeting: Inspirations from Above*. He recently co-authored with his eight-year-old son, E.J., a children's book, *Wonderfully Made and Exceptionally Gifted*. Sales are doing well, briefly reaching #1 on Amazon Christian children's books. That book and *Mentors Matter but Poverty Sucks*, aim to touch the lives of children and teens caught in the cycle of poverty. Society quickly labels children born into poverty "at-risk". Unfortunately for some, this label becomes branded into their identity, making the prospect of success seem unattainable. Therefore, the children's book uses the world of a kid's imagination to allow the reader to visualize that no child is without merit or talent. A child without positive affirmation is likely to perform beneath his potential — once adorable children become society's figurative punching bags as they stumble toward adulthood. This reality for many teens ascribed to poverty is the truest motivation for the book *Mentors Matter but Poverty Sucks* — it tells the gripping true stories experienced by teens labeled "at-risk".

Although Eugene received his doctorate, he is still expanding his knowledge by pursuing an MBA. He was recently accepted into the Emerging Leaders Cohort — at the University of Illinois at Urbana-Champaign, only eleven students were chosen from a pool of world applicants. Additionally, he was recruited through a highly selective process by Illinois Business Consulting (IBC) — the largest professionally-managed, student-run consulting organization of its kind, annually linking students to over 70 real-world projects from mid-sized startup companies, nonprofits and the Fortune 100. Through the university, he frequently visits some of the world's most elite schools. Most recently he traveled to Singapore, Paris, Rome, and Toronto, where he is able to collaboratively draw from them a deeper understanding of advances in educational systems and the global economy.

He understands that education can move a child from poverty to purpose, but in the absence of the opportunity for a quality education, these children are likely to become products of their environment. Without compromise or hesitation, he continues to make the investment in the lives of children, whom some have deemed lost causes because he knows no child is void of innate gifts. In addition to working for the University of Illinois at Urbana-Champaign, he serves as the President and Chief Executive Officer of Assurance Creek Youth Program, Inc. and as a consultant to various business enterprises. His latest books serve as examples of his commitment to using his gifts, talents, and resources to help others. Dr. Eugene L. Moore is simply a man on a mission to change the world one child at a time.

DEDICATION

You departed my life when I was a young child but through the miraculous power of God, you imparted such love to me that I would have to live an eternity to reciprocate it to the world. I vividly remember standing on the chair next to the stove, watching you intensely relishing every moment, as you made dinner. I recall being a willing taste-tester. I remember our frequent trips to the grocery store and small antique shops, and your willingness to reward my good behavior with ice cream. I so appreciated your stern yet gentle nature as it kept me on a straight path. You taught me how to pray, love, forgive, share and be a humble servant. I dedicate this book to Annie B. Moore, the uneducated southern woman from Isola, Mississippi who told me my shoulders were broad and my future was filled with endless possibilities. Your love has never escaped my grasp and continues to live today. You instinctively and prophetically knew your grandson would rise above the fray. So every time someone refers to me as Dr. Eugene L. Moore, my heart will smile because you believed in me first and prayed for my success. Your beauty, grace, and integrity are everlasting memories. I love you, grandma!

Acknowledgments

There are so many people I want to thank for their help to ensure my journey was filled with hope, optimism, feedback, and encouragement. I would be remiss if I did not take this opportunity to express my gratitude to those who imparted their wisdom and unwavering support. For those not mentioned by name, I am still deeply grateful to my many mentors, teachers, professors, colleagues and friends who selflessly offered their support and for that, I say thank you.

Associate Professor Yoon Pak was instrumental in her efforts to advise me through the process of completing my doctorate. She is the embodiment of a professional and understands the lives of graduate students are often filled with unforeseen circumstances and setbacks. She demonstrated compassion, sympathy, and empathy but not at the expense of letting me lose focus on the end goal of completing my graduate program. As an adviser, she laced up her shoes tightly and got in the race with me to ensure my success and for that, I say thank you.

Teaching Associate Professor Denice Ward Hood was a delight to have on my committee. She had a thorough intellectual approach that added great value to the scholarship and integrity of the study. In addition, she is genuinely a caring person wanting to assure her advisees, colleagues, family, and friends are well holistically and for that, I say thank you.

Associate Professor Christopher Span has long been an unofficial mentor. I deeply admire his intelligence and his historical lens on the hidden narratives of former slaves. He always provides encouragement and his mantra: "No Complaints" plays repeatedly in my mind. He received all of his degrees from Illinois and I followed in his footsteps. I am always delighted to see how this remarkable man interacts with his intellectually inquisitive son, Langston — perhaps because I come from a single-parent home without a father. I am always cognizant when I see a strong man providing a foundation of love and support for his family and for that, I say thank you.

The Dean of the College of Education and Gutgsell Professor, James D. Anderson has been an integral contributor to higher education with nearly 50 years. To surmise his value I am reminded of the late Dr. Martin Luther King Jr.'s prerecorded sermon, aimed to instruct the presiding minister during his eulogy. Instead, it was played at his funeral at the request of his widow, Coretta Scott King. It instructed: "Tell him not to mention that I have a Nobel Peace Prize — that isn't important. Tell him not to mention that I have 300 or 400 other awards — that's not important. Tell him not to mention where I went to school. I'd like somebody to mention that day that Martin Luther King Jr. tried to give his life serving others." In my estimation, James D. Anderson exemplifies what it means to be a servant and for that, I say thank you.

Professor Laurence Parker played a pivotal role in my pursuit to achieve a doctorate in Educational Policy Studies (EPS). In December 2009, I ran into him in the halls of the College of Education. He had stated earlier he would be out of the office for the majority of the day, so to be courteous and not infringe on his time, I kept my query/greeting brief. To my surprise, he responded that he had a few moments to talk. In that brief encounter, he introduced me to the Department of Educational Policy Studies, provided insightful advice, and gave me a copy of the Harvard Educational Review, which I voraciously read. I can unequivocally say this brief interaction was not serendipitous — it was the collision of ambition and opportunity for me and for that, I say thank you.

The University of Illinois at Urbana-Champaign is a world-renowned institution. But when I first walked on the quad in 1997, I was simply amazed at how so many students from all around the globe had converged there with a single mission — to be a part of the Illini family. I was happy, but not satisfied, to receive my Bachelor of Arts degree in 2001. In May 2003, I earned a Master of Education degree, after which I went to work in corporate America gaining many intangible skills from a Fortune 5 corporation and other leading companies. But I was restless and still found myself perplexed by the state of our educational system coupled with injustices many marginalized groups face. I returned to Illinois to pursue my Ph.D. in Educational Policy Studies (awarded in May 2017), so that I may affect solutions to the things that bother me — not just sing in the criticism choir. I have re-enrolled and will receive an M.B.A. in May 2019. This pursuit of higher education was never vainglorious, rather is based on my personal motivation to move beyond my ideological disposition and theoretical constraints so that I can develop and affect practical, pragmatic solutions. The U of I has provided me the platform to represent marginalized voices with integrity and scholarship and for that, I say thank you.

Since 1997 the Office of Minority Student Affairs (OMSA) has been a constant presence throughout my time at Illinois, providing me mentorship and needed resources to propel my academic achievement. Minority graduate students have the flexibility to break away from OMSA to move around campus and seek different opportunities which I most certainly did. Nonetheless, I remained committed to OMSA' invaluable work. As an undergraduate, they provided me a mentor. As a graduate student and academic professional, they let me be a mentor to pay it forward and for that, I say thank you.

For more than 20 years, I have witnessed Attorney and Judge Laurie June Samuels excel and give to others while balancing her other responsibilities-running her law firm, heading her retirement planning consulting firm, and being a judge. I am a benefactor of her selfless efforts. Her willingness to edit my research papers or write the forward in my second book, even though she was busy crafting a legal brief or memorandum, was astonishing. She is a dynamic counselor and an invaluable friend and for that, I say thank you.

James R. Moore, Deedee D. Moore, Nicole R. Moore, Devontae D. Moore, Trezorann D. Moore, Treyvon D. Moore, Rosie L. Williams and Edna M. Nash — God saw fit to make us family and for that, I say thank you.

Nikita, Elijah and Eugene L. Moore II (EJ) — you are the ones who listened to me read countless pages without complaining. You have experienced my frenetic states ranging from jubilation to extreme exhaustion, yet you never withheld your love or belief in me and for that, I say thank you.

Mother, Police Officer, and Friend — it is difficult to explain the impact you have on my life. I have repeatedly observed your resilience and vividly recall your countless sacrifices to ensure my future would have boundless opportunities. As a single-mother, you never complained about lack of support or made me feel as if I was at-risk because of my circumstances. This book focuses on the mentor-mentee relationship typically between a non-familial adult and a younger protégé. But in all honesty, you have been the master navigator on my figurative ship of life. You mentored and encouraged me to seek greatness. You gave me the courage to dream big and to be the captain of my own ship. But you were also wise enough to understand it takes a village, so you exposed me to great mentors, demanded I strive for excellence and instilled in me the importance of speaking articulately. You were my first writing coach for short narrative and poetry writing competitions at school, teaching and inspiring me to use my written words to speak truth to power. You insisted I stand up to injustice and never concede to fear. You dressed me as a toddler in suits because you saw a future for me demanding professional attire and leadership. You went so far as to tell me that with God I could do all things. You simply made me believe I was unstoppable and for that, I say thank you. I love you, mom!

The Father, Son, and Holy Spirit are my true place of refuge and serenity. I am a descendant of former slaves and my great-great-grandmother was a sharecropper. I remember my childhood clearly — my beliefs were no different than the average child. I believed in the Tooth Fairy and waited with expectation when I lost a tooth knowing that underneath my pillow would be a crisp dollar bill. I remember coloring many eggs in anticipation of the Easter Bunny. I remember waiting for the magical Santa Claus to descend down the chimney. And I remember my great-great grandmother telling me a story of this baby born in a manger — from that very moment my life as I knew it was forever changed. My mother recently read to me a note I had written as a child to God. I was both humbled and amazed. It was evident my belief in Christ was more intense than the magical nature of the Tooth Fairy, the Easter Bunny or Santa Claus, which I soon learned anyway were no more real than the bogeyman living under my bed. I have read in research articles, evidenced in slave narratives, how African-Americans are typically Christ followers. The vileness of slavery and the evilness of poverty are inherently void of hope unless you factor in God. He can dismantle any form of oppression. Father in Heaven you have bestowed such favor upon my life and for that, I say thank you.

Foreword

Over the course of nearly 30 years of practicing law, I have had the opportunity to mentor hundreds of young men and women. No mentee has stood out more to me than Dr. Eugene Moore. I first met Dr. Moore when he was a sixth-grade student at Brown Elementary School, located in the footprint of the Henry Horner Public Housing Development in Chicago, Illinois. I was teaching a class for Junior Achievement of Chicago and Dr. Moore was one of my students. His inquisitiveness and grasp of the subject matter immediately told me three things about him. First, Dr. Moore was determined to define his environment, rather than letting his environment define him. Yes, he lived in public housing, but he knew that public housing did not have to live in him. I could see even then that he was determined to become successful and make a tremendous impact on society.

Second, Dr. Moore loves learning. Even as a kid, he would constantly ask questions about the lessons I was teaching, my law practice, and a variety of other topics. I was not surprised in the least when he called and told me that he was going to pursue his Ph.D. from the University of Illinois. Learning is in his blood. He realized at an early age, that outside of God, education is the greatest equalizer in the world. It has allowed him to rise from public housing to become one of the most prolific young writers in the country.

Lastly, Dr. Moore recognizes the value of mentoring. From our initial meeting decades ago until now, Dr. Moore has stayed in touch with me. He regularly checks in with me and keeps me updated about the various important events going on in his life. I was excited when he reached out to me and told me he was writing a book on the importance of mentoring because I knew he truly understood the subject matter.

Simply put, mentoring can be the difference between a child rising above his or her environment and a child succumbing to his or her environment. This book is full of pearls of wisdom on the subject and is a must-read for anyone who truly wants to learn about the importance of this critical subject.

Samuel Mendenhall, J.D.

Winston & Strawn LLP

Author's Message of Hope

I will spare you the details about my upbringing as it is intricately woven throughout the book but do know my story is not far from the many teens who I interviewed and observed for this study. Poverty, crime and violence are largely systemic issues and many young African American teens are in the midst of a horror film starring themselves. Often times when we turn on the television or read our social media feed we are inundated with stories of hopelessness. African American children murdered in the streets sometimes because of an over-aggressive police officer, gang violence, abusive parents or just as an innocent bystander. In no way should we indict the countless brave police officers who risk their lives daily to protect the citizens of their respective communities but to ignore the unconscious and conscious bias displayed by some which result in the loss of life of unarmed African Americans is a grave misstep of justice.

Many politicians, judges, lawyers, celebrities, scholars, ministers, school districts, community members, parents and even children tune in for their daily dose of carnage but who will have the courage to change the channel and the narrative. History has produced such great leaders like the late Dr. Martin Luther King Jr. to those who are less known but their tenacity to rewrite the stories of injustice speak volumes. It is time we destroy the labels of at-risk, low-income and single-parent which at best is coded language for those who some believe are destined to fail. It is perplexing and downright deplorable that we as a nation have a great indication of how the story of poverty, violence and poor education ends but instead of offering solutions some continue to turn a blind eye toward the perpetual horror they continuously indulge. It is my greatest hope that teens will read this book and come to learn they are no more at-risk than someone who lives in a gated community but what separates them is their extreme poverty which seems to impart its vileness upon those most vulnerable. It is time to get up from the dismal feature film of your life and not be a stationary target.

African American teens all around the world I have a secret, those systemic issues like poverty, gun violence and high dropout rates tried to target me as well and even with the unwavering support of family and mentors their tenacity was relentless but I learned to believe in my success more than a system that bet on my failure. The African American teen who wears loafers and a cardigan sweater is no less of a target than the teen who wears Timberland boots and a hoodie because what is truly under attack is your potential, not your wardrobe. I encourage you to get up from this socially constructed label called at-risk which subconsciously and consciously screams to you that you are deficient. I was targeted because you did not want me to realize my potential. When I am given equal and equitable opportunity I am much more than an athlete or an entertainer but I am the same person you once claimed to adore at three years old.

As I grew older your interactions changed and the labels began. I am not your free and reduced lunch, individualized education program, future inmate or at-risk student but I am a child of God with endless possibilities. My hope is that African American teens do not define themselves by their ascribed circumstances or the labels which have been conveniently used to describe their disposition and social condition but instead I implore you to be resilient to withstand the bullseye that has been intentionally and disingenuously placed upon your back and when you one day walk across the stage to receive a post-secondary degree you can boldly say, "I guess you missed the target." When life presents you an obstacle and trust me it indeed will please hold on to the message my grandmother and mother both taught me which is, "With man this is impossible, but with God, all things are possible" Matthew 19:26 NIV.

—Eugene L. Moore, Ph.D.

Eugene L. Moore, Ph.D.

Research suggests more than three million young people, a large majority of them considered at-risk, are engaged in some type of mentoring relationship. "At-risk is a term typically used to describe youth who struggle with the realities of poverty, including those growing up in single-parent homes, those with emotional or behavioral problems and those living in high crime and violent neighborhoods." (Keating, Tomishima, Foster, & Alessandri, 2002).

PREFACE

Although mentoring programs have received strong endorsements from federal, state and local governments for decades, what do we truly know about their effectiveness? Mentoring is indeed widely accepted as a low-cost intervention for vulnerable populations specifically aimed at curtailing school dropout rates, violence and crime. But what is its impact on poverty? In all actuality, school dropout rates, violence and crime are all direct consequences of poverty. Should we continue to use mentoring programs as a bandage for the gaping wound poverty creates or should we make a valiant attempt to break the poverty cycle in one of the richest nations on the planet? The question on all accounts is rhetorical because failure to address poverty as the culprit is senseless. When we place a face on poverty, do we see people as less worthy of receiving opportunities? Be advised poverty is colorblind. This book focuses on the lives of 10 African-American teens, all unaware what it means to be at-risk — literally and figuratively caught in the crossfire fire of poverty despite having mentors.

Chapter 1
Introduction to the Research

This book examines the widely used intervention of mentoring, focusing on the predominant demographic for interventions—African-American at-risk youth. Mentoring, besides being commonly used, has also been highly researched, so the introduction's goal is to address how this particular study adds value to the field. The research provides a novel analysis of mentoring because its investigation is from the unique perspective of at-risk youth, who were selected to receive mentoring during an after-school program. In addition, it provides a detailed explanation of how the study was conducted. The introduction has four sections:1) statement of the problem, 2) purpose, and rationale for the study, 3) primary research and interview questions, and 4) organization of the study.

Statement of the Problem

While a doctoral student, my peers, colleagues, and faculty frequently asked the same question, "What is your research focus? "In the early stages of graduate study, I found this question to be somewhat overwhelming. I realized the focus would likely change — many other scholars and graduate students had warned this, relaying how their own research had evolved and taken completely different trajectories than they had originally imagined. Not only was the question problematic, but it also created some anxiety. Initially, I emphatically wanted to explore diversity beyond the convoluted rhetoric surrounding this heavily debated topic, but discovered instantly the topic was too broad. By the time the research focus narrowed sufficiently, it had morphed into a completely different topic.

Coming from a single-parent home and attending a subpar elementary school, I was introduced at an early age to mentoring and its benefits. My mother was intentional in her approach to expose me to positive non-familial male role models, in an effort to combat some of the harsh realities surrounding my community like poverty, gun violence, and high dropout rates. Reflection on my upbringing began to inform my newfound research focus on the mentor-mentee relationship and created a litany of questions about this readily used intervention called mentoring. Questions like: "What is mentoring?" "What makes mentoring an effective intervention for at-risk African-American youth?" "What are the lasting effects of the mentor-mentee relationship?" Truthfully, these questions were only a fraction of the questions consuming my inquiring mind. Not only did I grapple with these questions, but I was also trying to understand my success, both academically and professionally — I was always disconcerted by those who deemed meritocracy as the reason for my success, completely ignoring the inherent challenges I had faced and overcame.

Often times those individuals never questioned why so many of my peers, despite their efforts and dreams, voluntarily and sometimes involuntarily, succumbed to the disheartening realities the community exhibited. Thus, while mentoring was an effective intervention for me, it was not for most of my peers. The notion that I worked hard and because of my efforts alone, I achieved success, is preposterous. I contend my success is a culmination of many factors like supportive family, spiritual intuitiveness, resilience, good teachers, mentors and other influential circumstances helping propel my accomplishments. So as I began to unpack my research topic, I knew I needed to define mentoring coupled with using qualitative methods to explore the varied lived experiences of African-American youth in urban communities. One of the first things I had to come to terms with was what it means to be labeled "at-risk".

Research suggests more than three million young people, a large majority of them considered at-risk, are engaged in some type of mentoring relationship. "At-risk is a term typically used to describe youth who struggle with the realities of poverty, including those growing up in single-parent homes, those with emotional or behavioral problems and those living in high crime and violent neighborhoods." (Keating, Tomishima, Foster, & Alessandri, 2002). As a youth I did not feel at-risk nor did I realize the constraints of being reared in a single-parent home. Upon reflection, it was apparent that my mother was more than aware of these realities. She instinctively believed exposing me to successful African-American males through mentorship would help me escape the pillars of failure surrounding my community. Rhodes (2002) defines mentoring as a "relationship between an older, more experienced adult and an unrelated younger protégé — a relationship in which the adult provides ongoing guidance, instruction and encouragement aimed at developing the competence and character of the protégé"(p. 3).

In retrospect, I had great mentors who exposed me to numerous positive experiences such as Junior Achievement, Illinois Student Forum, golf outings and even employment at top corporations, Citigroup and Merrill Lynch. But my experience was simply that — my experience. I recall sitting in Heathrow Airport with my mentor of nearly 20 years and listening to him explain how mine was the only successful mentor-mentee relationship he had fostered despite offering the same level of support to other mentees. This reality has played repeatedly in my mind and has undergirded my research to expose the varied experiences of mentees. The majority of my experience with mentors took place after school. The time between school dismissal and late evening is extremely hazardous for at-risk youth. Unless students are engaged in extracurricular activities like sports, clubs or mentor-mentee focused activities, they are more than likely hanging out and engaging in non-productive activities. Hence, national organizations — like the YMCA, Boys and Girls Club of America, and Big Brother and Big Sisters (BBBS) — and local organizations like churches, all play pivotal roles in keeping at-risk youth off the streets. In light of my lived experience, I gravitated toward researching the mentor-mentee relationship as it unfolds in an after-school program situated in a micro-urban neighborhood amid the gripping circumstances of the surrounding community.

Purpose and Rationale for Research Study

My lived experience (having mentors since I was five years old) was extremely positive and contributed to my success. But the purpose of this study draws on why my lived experience is not indicative of all mentor-mentee relationships. The preponderance of research suggests mentoring relationships are primarily positive, especially for those youth considered at-risk. In fact, mentors serve as a critical support system for children deemed at-risk as a result of poverty and other debilitating social factors (J. Christiansen, J. L. Christiansen, and Howard, 1997). Hence, children's exposure to positive adults or even peers has proven an effective strategy to deal with challenges. In addition to providing children with productive alternatives to handle tough circumstances, the mentor-mentee relationship can make achieving success more probable. However, as I began to unpack the complexities of mentoring, I soon realized it was important to understand the lived experiences of mentees irrespective of the notion that mentor-mentee relationships generally have favorable outcomes. Even though we see strong endorsements of mentoring programs from communities, school districts, and the federal government, when I reflect on my own experience juxtaposed with that of my peers, I am left with many unanswered questions.

In seventh grade, we had a new teacher from California who was simply exceptional. Despite her father's disapproval, she had traveled nearly 2,000 miles in her Ford Escort to make a difference in the inner city of Chicago. The Chicago Public Schools (CPS) were well-known for delivering substandard academic outcomes, especially for those students who resided in poverty-stricken neighborhoods; but what perhaps troubled her father more was the high concentration of crime and violence surrounding the school. One day when heading home after school, our teacher was severely injured (she tore her anterior cruciate ligament — ACL) while trying to aid a dog that had been struck by an automobile. She had to undergo emergency surgery and was in the hospital for more than a week. A few of us visited her in the hospital and got to meet her parents. Her mother was a loving, nurturing person. But, her father was aloof, did not speak and quickly exited the room when we entered. It was at that time our teacher revealed to us her father's strong disregard for African-Americans and vehement disapproval of her teaching in the Chicago inner city. Unaffected by her father's disdain, she intuitively understood the importance of exposing her students to positive, non-familial adults; and she went well beyond her responsibility to fill the role model and learning gaps so many students faced.

Sadly, many children enter school with inadequate preparation, unaddressed learning disabilities, and/or various behavioral, emotional and social developmental issues that increase their risk of school-related problems. Urban youths are particularly vulnerable to school problems because of challenges associated with urban poverty (Broussard, Mosley-Howard, & Roychoudhury, 2006). In spite of developing deep, lifelong relationships with her students, our teacher felt that as a privileged white woman her impact would be limited, not because of a lack of empathy or compassion but because no matter how hard she addressed the stark realities of the inner city, she would never fully understand what it meant to be black in America. While she felt it was easier to connect with the girls in the classroom, she believed the boys would be better served by successful African-American male mentors. So, for the boys, she sought the support of African-American male mentors through the Junior Achievement Program.

The initial two mentors were remarkable men — one had grown up in public housing and had risen to the rank of Junior Partner at one of the world's top law firms and the other, a Vice President of a Fortune 500 company. I remember that day vividly. As I watched them in awe, I instinctively knew my current circumstances were not going to negatively impact my future. However, despite the eagerness of these men to make a difference, only three African-American boys decided to fully engage in the mentor-mentee relationship. In retrospect, my teacher's hospital stay was probably a major turning point for her — when she witnessed the racism and implicit bias from her own father against her young students, she realized how these societal attitudes could hinder African-Americans' academic achievement. As a consequence, she continually sought the help of mentors to combat this deplorable reality.

The purpose and rationale for this research were guided by the outcomes of these three boys from nearly 25 years ago. If my research pool included only the three boys, then the success rate of the mentoring relationship would have been 33%. If it was expanded to include those who had the opportunity, but did not participate, then it would drop to roughly 5%. Although success is relative, this outcome seems beyond subpar, since the program was introduced specifically as a positive intervention to curtail the realities of urban poverty. Despite the many studies strongly reporting the effectiveness of mentoring, I am still compelled to ask some pertinent questions relating to my own experience in elementary school — why was the mentoring program, anchored by two highly accomplished African-American males, insufficient to overcome the barriers of poverty and learned helplessness? Why did so many young and impressionable boys opt out of the mentoring program? Why did the same opportunities and exposure afforded my two peers and me result in such different outcomes — with only me managing to escape the encapsulating unhealthy environment? To answer these questions, I set out to unpack the mentor-mentee relationship (beyond its popularity of being an effective intervention for at-risk youth) to discover how mentoring is experienced from the viewpoint of the mentee. To add my own scholarship to the already robust research on mentoring, I focused not only on those who had successful mentor-mentee relationships, but also those who had not, to explain why their experiences did not garner success. Through the varied lived experiences of mentees, I uncovered what needs to happen to produce more favorable outcomes.

Research Questions and Interview Questions

Mentoring, the purpose of which is to help at-risk youths cope with their circumstances, is a commonplace in-school intervention tool. Schools frequently use mentoring as an intervention for at-risk students and look to pair them with individuals who can hopefully provide guidance and help them build self-esteem coupled with a high level of resiliency (Converse and Lignugaris-Kraft 2009). Mentoring is virtually ubiquitous in after-school programs with high numbers of at-risk youth in attendance in communities similar to Prairie Urban. Perhaps poverty is the impetus driving the ready use of mentoring programs as interventions. In order to cope with and/or combat the circumstances poverty presents, it is necessary to both create productive activity and prevent nonproductive activity when school is not in session. The overarching research questions guiding the study are as follows:

RQ1: How can mentor-mentee relationships provide a positive and/or effective alternative for at-risk youth to combat systemic issues like poverty, gun violence, and high dropout rates?

RQ2: How are non-familial relationships like the dyadic relationship of the mentor-mentee perceived from the mentee's perspective?

During the semi-formal interview process, the following questions were asked of the participants to help guide the conversation about their lived experiences as it relates to the mentor-mentee relationship(s):

1) Tell me about yourself as it relates to your upbringing?
2) How do you see the community in which you currently live?
3) What is mentoring?
4) What has been your previous experience with mentoring programs?
5) Please share when you were first introduced to mentoring and how did you feel about having a mentor?
6) How long have you been coming to the Community Youth Center?
7) Why do you come to the Community Youth Center?

8) What programs or activities are you involved in at the Community Youth Center?

9) What do you consider a good mentor-mentee relationship?

10) What do you consider a bad mentor-mentee relationship?

11) Do you have a preference of whom you would like to be your mentor? For example, do they need to be the same race, ethnicity or gender?

12) How do you like the Extend-a-Hand Program?

13) When you hear the term "at-risk", what immediately comes to your mind and how does it make you feel?

14) What are your short-term goals and how do you plan to achieve them over the next year?

15) What are your long-term goals and how do you plan to achieve them over the next 2-5 years?

16) How do you value mentor relationships?

17) How are mentor relationships different or similar to the relationships you have with family members like parents, siblings, cousins, etc.?

18) If you had a good relationship with your mentor how likely would you share some of your innermost thoughts and feelings?

19) How likely do you believe your mentor can relate to your upbringing and be effective in understanding your circum-

stances or what you are going through?

20) How safe is the neighborhood where the Community Youth Center is located?

21) Do you believe the Community Youth Center helps to reduce crime, violence and dangerous activity in the community?

22) How comfortable would you be to invite your mentor to your home and how comfortable would you be to visit his/her home?

23) What is the most positive experience you have had with your mentor and what is the most disappointing?

24) Do you believe your mentor has the capacity to help you escape the realities of your circumstances?

25) What person has inspired you the most and why? (Your response can be family, friends, or people you have never formally met.)

These questions elicited personalized accounts of how the mentor-mentee relationship is viewed from the perspective of the mentee. They guided the discussions nicely beyond the consensus conclusion of mentoring being an effective intervention for at-risk youth. The participants' ages ranged from 13 to 18 years old. At times the questions were not clearly understood, so they were reworded to account for the varying levels of education and/or maturity.

In addition to interviewing the participants, the Director of Operations gave me permission to question staff about programmatic functions of the Extend-a-Hand Program and other pertinent information needed to inform the study. The questions I asked staff members follow:

1) What are your name, title and current role at the Community Youth Center?

2) What is your educational background?

3) What made you decide to join the Community Youth Center?

4) What are your goals for the members you serve?

5) What is your definition of mentoring?

6) What is your definition of at-risk?

7) What are the biggest challenge and the greatest reward of working with members of the Community Youth Center?

8) What are the primary issues or circumstances members face? How do you help address those issues?

9) Explain the Extend-a-Hand Program and its structure?

10) Explain how mentors are selected for the Extend-a-Hand Program and what, if any formal training they receive prior to meeting with their mentees?

11) How do you develop and/or oversee programs? How do you measure their success?

12) Have you been a mentor or mentee and if so, explain your experience?

These questions posed to staff, along with the interviews of the participants, inform the study.

Organization of the Study

Chapter two provides a literature review of the theoretical framework of mentoring — a comprehensive discussion ranging from the history of mentoring to the challenges the intervention presents — to impart some foundational insight into the topic. Chapter three discusses the research design and methodological approach. Chapter four includes the findings from the interviews and observations of the thirteen participants (10 youth and 3 staff members). Chapter five discusses and analyzes data derived from the primary research questions. Chapter six reviews the conclusions of the study and provides implications and suggestions for future research because it is crucial to continue the quest for deeper understanding.

Chapter 2
Literature Review

Introduction

Mentoring is a broad topic. In order to properly understand its complexity, it is useful to be cognizant of its main reoccurring themes. The literature review begins with defining the term "at-risk". The term has almost proven synonymous when defining mentorship in the context of micro-urban communities. After gaining an understanding of what "at-risk" signifies, the study explores ten subcategories: 1) the history of mentoring, 2) key components of effective mentoring programs, 3) mentoring structure and programming, 4) resiliency, 5) race, ethnicity, and gender, 6) competitive versus at-risk students, 7) college students and elders as mentors, 8) challenges of mentoring, 9) negative effects of mentoring, and 10) Mentee Perspectives.

The history of mentoring provides a concise yet thorough account of how mentorship has become a readily used intervention. The key components of effective mentoring outline the infrastructure of an ideal program. Mentoring structure and programming provide insights into what we know about mentoring programs and their design. The section on resiliency provides some insight into what it means to be resilient and how mentoring can bolster resiliency — a term heavily correlated to at-risk African-American youth and their ability to withstand challenging circumstances. Race, ethnicity, and gender form a contentious relationship surrounding mentoring — some believe only same race, same ethnicity and same gender offer the necessary platform for a positive mentor-mentee relationship. The comparison between highly competitive versus at-risk students offers another interesting perspective on mentorship. Exploring how college students and retired people often serve as mentors — and the challenges both populations present — adds value to the dichotomous relationship of mentoring. It is equally important to understand the negative effects the intervention can cause for both the mentor and mentee. The literature review would be lacking if it did not include mentee perspectives. These ten subcategories, while appearing disjointed, offer a multifaceted, unique look at the field of mentoring.

AT-RISK YOUTH

Two troubling realities for many at-risk youth are the scarcity of volunteer resources, and although mentoring receives favorable acclaim, those most likely to be effective mentors are busy (Hamilton, 2010). This scarcity exists because the demand is simply greater than the supply, as the rise in single-parent households has vastly increased, coupled with poorly resourced communities and smaller extended families (Hartley, 2004). Although research has proven the benefits of a mentor-mentee relationship, scarcity of counselors can simply overshadow any potential results. Nonetheless, having an older, more experienced adult to advise and encourage youth will continue to be a readily used intervention. It is this dynamic that makes mentorship such an important intervention for at-risk youth — it builds relationships that in most cases would not otherwise have been formed. Yet this example highlights the chronic challenges most at-risk children still face:

> Children in today's schools bring with them diverse learning, behavioral, emotional, and social needs as they enter the school

door. With the use of effective teaching practices and well-developed support services, the needs of many of these students are met routinely in the school environment. However, there are still children who are at-risk for school failure primarily due to such factors as environmental stresses, chronic school failure, and abuse and neglect. To meet the needs of these students, schools need multifaceted approaches (Christiansen, Christiansen and Howard, 1997).

These realities add credence to the need for strong mentoring programs that can help establish relationships that give a sense of belonging to at-risk youth. Unfortunately, many at-risk youth become lost in the educational system, especially when they are placed in special education courses. One of the negative side-effects of Special Ed is that it often makes student feels isolated and ostracized, even leading to their eventual drop out basically to escape the non-nurturing classroom setting. Fortunately, when a child is paired with a committed mentor before he is overwhelmed by circumstances, the result can be beneficial and in many cases life-changing. Christiansen, Christiansen, and Howard (1997) define the benefits of mentors stating:

> Mentors serve as critical support for children at-risk as a result of poverty, trauma, substance abuse, or other life events. Children who have a significant attachment to or a bond with an adult, or sometimes another child, tend to face their challenges more productively and are more likely to experience success.

Mentorship has a robust history laced with both benefits and burdens. Since its introduction, it has been heavily focused on mitigating some of the social ills that plague many urban areas across America.

History of Mentoring

Although mentoring has existed for over a century, it has only been in the past 20 years or so that researchers have highlighted its prevalence. Mentoring is the matching of a responsible adult with a young person who may benefit from such a relationship. While mentor-mentee relationships are sometimes familial ones, it is typically an unrelated adult who volunteers their time and resources to the mentoring program or initiative (Pryce, 2012). Mentoring programs come in many different forms — school, community, and faith-based — offering natural and program-based variations in how mentoring is delivered. Faith-based organizations play a key role in serving vulnerable populations. Churches will host events like block parties, cookouts, and others activities aimed to keep at-risk youth off the streets. Although these community-hosted events have the potential to attract youth, it is still important to connect them with positive mentors to foster the environment that may rewrite their life chances.

The realities many youth face create a huge demand for mentor relationships outside of the home to provide guidance and encouragement (Randolph and Johnson, 2008). Given the influx of attention toward mentoring, it has been defined by many researchers and scholars. Rhodes (2002) defines mentoring as a "relationship between an older, more experienced adult and an unrelated younger protégé- a relationship in which the adult provides ongoing guidance, instruction, and encouragement aimed at developing the competence and character of the protégé" (p.3). A mentor is traditionally defined as someone who is older by 8 to 15 years than their mentee. Mentors typically take parental roles in which they provide mentees with teaching and feedback about prospective career and personal life circumstances (Day, 2006). Moodie and Fisher

(2009) define mentoring as, "the commitment of time and specific efforts by a more experienced person to the development of a mutually beneficial, supportive and nurturing relationship with a less experienced person" (p. 41). While there are many definitions of mentoring there seems to be a common thread among them — an older adult with more experience than their younger counterpart. The mentor's goal is to provide a meaningful relationship characterized by their experiences and serve as a positive role model (VanderVen, 2004). The interest and appeal of mentoring are not surprising as it is a low-cost intervention that utilizes local resources and caring individuals to assist at-risk youth. Mentoring programs generally have some flexibility in structuring so it can be altered to meet a variety of needs. In recent years, federal government funding of mentoring initiatives is accounting for the increase in new programs (J. Miller, Barnes, H. Miller and Mckinnon, 2012). Given the extreme interest in mentoring as an intervention, researchers are beginning to unpack the programmatic infrastructure to determine its effectiveness. Furthermore, it is equally important to develop a clear expectation of key components necessary to ensure an effective mentoring program.

Key Components of Effective Mentoring Programs

Throughout literature, the positive effects of mentoring for at-risk youth, making it the "go to" intervention, are well documented. But for effectiveness, some key components are imperative — aimlessly targeting at-risk youth without adhering to some key principles would elicit a poor outcome at the expense of the vulnerable child. An obvious component needed is the ability to establish a strong bond between the mentor and mentee which is best achieved when the relationship is maintained over a long period of time (Rhodes, 2002). Given this factor is maintained, it enhances the chances that at-risk youths have to improve their academics and social behavior. Mentoring is an activity frequently driven by someone's passion to help vulnerable populations. But passion, devoid of training, is a sure way to attract failure. Herrera et al. (2013) believe mentors who receive early match training and support from their program staff have a better chance to enhance the mentor-mentee relationship. Early match training provides the mentor with clear and reasonable expectations of the mentor-mentee relationship coupled with delivering an understanding of the mentee's responsibility. This support is not disjointed but extensive and provides mentors with the necessary tools to develop mentor-mentee relationships without feeling as if they are tackling the intervention in isolation. In addition to establishing a bond with the mentee and providing quality training for the prospective mentor, it is also equally important to develop a relationship with the parents of the at-risk youth. Dortch (as cited by Jackson 2003) contends communication between the mentor and the parent(s) or guardian(s) is essential to maintaining a strong mentor-mentee relationship. It is up to the mentor to establish a relationship with the mentee; but when that relationship is strongly supported and encouraged by the parent or guardian, it makes the ability to foster such a relationship less cumbersome.

It is essential for mentors to have passion and commitment to do the valuable work of mentoring, but without extensive training, screening, support of program staff and parental support their efforts may have little to no impact. Rhodes (2002) contends when programs lack the infrastructure of screening, training and mentor support, the chances for a successful mentor-mentee relationship are greatly diminished. Thus, the potential to use mentoring programs to curtail poor behavior and improve academic performance is threatened when the program has not adhered to these essential components that leave the mentor less equipped to establish a meaningful mentor-mentee relationship. The next section explores how the structure and design of mentoring programs play an essential role in ensuring mentor-mentee relationships can produce successful outcomes.

Mentoring Structure and Programming

As communities, school districts and parents seek mentor programs, more scrutiny is placed on the structuring components of the program and its effectiveness. Programs may include cross-age peer mentoring, intergenerational mentoring, e-mentoring and group mentoring. However, each of these structures presents its own levels of success and challenges (Karcher, Kuperminc, Portwood, Sipe and Taylor, 2006).

Despite these programmatic issues, mentoring continues to be the go-to intervention for some of the most vulnerable youth. J. Miller, Barnes, H. Miller and Mckinnon (2012) state, "Estimates put the current number of programs and youth population served at more than 5,000 and approximately 3 million, respectively" (p. 440). Meyer and Bouchey (2010) offer common themes of successful mentoring programs. First, successful mentoring programs are not random acts, but are situation-focused and target the most vulnerable youth. Secondly, mentoring relationships, lasting a minimum of a year or longer, have a more successful impact than those mentoring relationships operating for shorter periods. Thirdly, the socioeconomic background of the mentor plays a role in the mentor-mentee relationship, as studies show mentors from higher income levels have more flexibility in their schedules, affording them more time to spend with the mentee. Lastly, successful programs match mentors with mentees of similar race, gender, and interests and set clear expectations. Mentoring structures generally include site-based or community-based activities held at schools, faith-based organizations or local service entities. Some of the nationally based programs like Big Brothers Big Sisters, Boys and Girls Club of America and United Way utilize a one-to-one mentor structure (J. Miller, Barnes, H. Miller and Mckinnon, 2012). Anatasia, Skinner and Mundhenk (2012) offer three layers of mentoring which deal with the type of connection (natural or assigned), setting (community-based or school-based) and intent (development or prescriptive) of the mentoring relationship. By selecting one component from each pairing, there are eight different combinations. For instance, natural community-based developmental (NCD) means a mentor and mentee will meet under organic conditions, their focus will likely be on more cognitive and social-emotional outcomes, and their activities will more likely be youth-driven and activity focused. Whether a mentor is assigned to a mentee or the interactions form naturally is unimportant. The only way to ensure positive outcomes is to make sure that the mentoring services align with the needs of youth. Because the use of mentoring programs is now commonplace, it is necessary that these programs and structures are assessed for their effectiveness.

It is equally important to understand what conditions render the greatest outcomes (Rhodes and Spencer, 2010). Furthermore, it is important to expose some of the complexities of the field — cognizance of the potential shortcomings of mentorship can ultimately better serve youth. Although at-risk youth are typically lumped together, not all of them are a good fit for mentoring. Despite it seeming insensitive to suggest an at-risk youth cannot benefit from a mentor relationship, such relationships do not eliminate the need for professional treatment for youth experiencing severe emotional, behavioral and academic problems. Thus, mentoring is not an all-inclusive remedy for at-risk youth (Rhodes and Spencer 2010). Perhaps mentoring has been deemed appealing to many organizations because it is highly attractive to funding sources within the private sector (Philip and Hendry, 2000). Two points are important — 1) not allowing the consensus of mentoring's effectiveness to cloud one's judgment and 2) finding any contentment in knowing some children will not benefit from the intervention. However, even the most effective program cannot account for all the children who become victims of systemic issues outside of their control.

The rapid growth in mentoring programs across the United States is largely due to the belief it is an effective intervention for at-risk youth. However, research has been mixed and little research has been done to assess the effectiveness of mentoring programs (Keating et al., 2002). Thus, theory and research have to play a pivotal role in the development and growth of interventions to provide merit for the relationships forged through mentoring programs (Rhodes and DuBois, 2008). The structure of mentoring programs is a critical part of developing quality outcomes. Another major theme in relation to mentoring is resiliency. Ideally, program leaders try to create safe spaces for youth to learn and develop the resiliency they need to survive their daily challenges. In fact, some argue it takes a great deal of resilience and determination to overcome the systemic pitfalls of poverty.

Resiliency

Mentoring has become commonplace as an in-school intervention with the purpose of helping at-risk youth cope with their circumstances. Schools frequently use mentoring as an intervention for at-risk students and look to pair them with individuals who can hopefully provide guidance and help them build self-esteem coupled with a high level of resiliency (Converse and Lignugaris-Kraft 2009). For some adults, resiliency is their mantra — they have overcome some troubling circumstances and sharing their stories with at-risk youth serves as a route on their own roadmap to escape failure. This interaction serves a dual purpose as it can empower youth and give the caring adult a sense of pride for his societal contributions (Brown, 2004). Day (2006) defines resiliency (using the definition cited in Newman 2002) as, "A positive adaptation where difficulties — personal, familial, or environmental — are so extreme that society otherwise would expect a person's cognitive or functional abilities to be impaired" (p. 196). VanderVen (2004) defines resilience as "the ability to adapt to adverse life consequences in a healthy way and is a major rationale for current youth development practices that encourage attributes, such as interests and social skills that increase coping skills" (p. 94). J. Christiansen, J. L. Christiansen and Howard (1997) define resilience as, "the ability to respond actively and positively to life conditions, stress, and trauma in such a way that we are able to bounce back and continue to approach life with positive actions" (p. 86). Unfortunately, because at-risk youth are forced to deal with a litany of uncontrollable issues, like poverty as its consequences of high concentrations of crime, they need resilience daily. Another consideration when measuring the effectiveness of mentoring programs is how race, ethnicity and gender factor into the mentor-mentee relationship.

RACE, ETHNICITY, AND GENDER

Because mentoring is a common intervention for at-risk youth who typically reside in urban areas with a high concentration of minorities, race is a factor in matching mentees with mentors. When structuring successful mentoring programs pairing mentors and mentees of similar race, gender, and interests are standard. But there still remains a debate whether matching mentees with mentors of the same race is actually more effective. Those opposed to cross-race matching argue that racial minorities will have a better connection with someone who has experienced racism. In addition, some suggest there is an inherent cultural mistrust of white mentors when paired with at-risk minority youth. Perhaps mentees will perceive feedback as bias due to the lack of cultural sensitivity. Despite these arguments, research has produced mixed findings whether race or ethnicity negatively affects the mentor-mentee relationship (Lee, Germain, Lawerence, and Marshall, 2010). It is also important for at-risk youth to have greater exposure to positive role models outside of professional sports and the entertainment industry. Mentorship is important for students who stand to gain insight into the importance of working hard. It is a gross mischaracterization that those equipped with talent achieve success without demonstrating a strong work ethic. Thus, at-risk students need to expand their role models to include more than athletes or entertainers, but scientist, doctors, and engineers. This reshaping of their outlook of success becomes a key purpose of the mentor-mentee relationship (Dawson, 2009).

Future research needs to explore the implications of race, culture, and ethnicity on mentoring as understanding their implications is only in the infancy stage. Specificity is needed to develop a hypothesis about how race, culture, or ethnicity influences the mentoring relationship. Such research would ultimately benefit the vast number of programs and the youth in which they serve (Darling et al., 2006). It is a common theme to discuss race when talking about mentorship as many of the programs were implemented to combat social ills that typically affect minority at-risk youth. In addition to social interactions that focus on race, ethnicity, and gender, disadvantaged youth also have to deal with their counterparts as it relates to their socio-economic differences —creating more disparities in opportunities. The determining factors for a youth being considered "at-risk" range from living in a single-parent home to living in abject poverty. These unique challenges place them at an even greater disadvantage compared to more affluent youths.

COMPETITIVE STUDENTS AND AT-RISK YOUTH

Most middle-class children have a commitment from their parents to expose them to a level of competitiveness to prepare them for their futures. Internalizing the importance of winning, developing a strategy to learn from failures, organizational and time-management skills, managing stress and the ability to receive feedback are key factors in building social capital. Middle-class parents are keenly aware of the benefits and innately impart these beliefs to their children to retain their place in society and secure a competitive advantage (Friedman, 2013). Because this reality is commonplace for middle-class families, it places at-risk youth at an even greater disadvantage compared to their more affluent counterparts. However, the guidance of middle-class parents, though appearing far more advanced, does not always produce stellar results. In fact, middle-class children are often self-centered, lack flexibility, lack resiliency, find themselves depending on their parents to right their wrongs, and have a high incidence of emotional immaturity. As it relates to leaders of the future they lack interpersonal skills and often confuse effort with excellence and quantity with quality (Levine and Dean, 2012). This debate over the parenting style and motivation of middle-class parents and the effectiveness of this style distract us from the issues at-risk youth face. It is likely their homes are void of caring adults accessible to advocate for their future. Talking about overzealous competitive kids or the overconfident college students are distractions.

Because a lack of positive influences creates a higher level of vulnerability for at-risk youth, mentorship serves as a needed component in their development. In the United States, approximately 25% of all youth and 50% of minority youth live in households headed by single-parents. Some parents work long hours, consequently leaving the children at home without adult supervision or interaction. The isolation the youth experiences often decreases the number of positive relationships they have with adults. These realities fuel the demand for and interest in mentoring programs. All children need to feel a sense of belonging. In most cases, this is provided by parents and extended family but sometimes, due to uncontrollable circumstances, they fail to adequately meet the needs of their children. Single-parents have to work as they are the sole providers for their children. This consequently removes them from the home and although extended family appears to be an option it is not always available (Anatasia, Skinner, and Mundhenk, 2012). These realities make mentoring a needed resource for children who face many obstacles and stand to gain a positive influence from a dedicated mentor who can potentially fill the void of an absent parent or guardian. This persistent reality makes after-school mentoring programs feasible solutions for youth who would otherwise be home alone. When mentoring is merged with tutoring, it can help at-risk students. However, mentoring largely focuses on relationship building and centers on academic achievement (Shepard, 2009). The goals for many mentoring programs are admirable, but given the high demand for mentors, organizations must explore the resources of nontraditional mentors to cover the shortfall. Failure to acknowledge the need to fill mentoring gaps and to provide feasible solutions will force many at-risk youth to contend with their struggles without the support of a caring adult.

College Students and Elders as Mentors

Despite the fact there is more than three million youth participating in mentoring, there is constant need to attract and develop more mentors. In some cases, prospective mentees wait a year or more before they are assigned a mentor. As a result, some programs recruit college students to contend with the shortage as they typically have more free time than working adults. However, because of the transitory nature of college students, some do not believe it is a dependable resource pool (Lee, Germain, Lawerence, and Marshall, 2010). Having a positive relationship with an adult outside the home often proves to be a protective factor for at-risk youth who are dealing with physiological and environmental changes, but the challenge entails securing a dependable adult who can meet the needs of the youth (Leyton-Armakan, Lawrence, Deutsch, Williams, and Henneberger, 2012). Thus, elder mentors especially those with similar experiences can be effective for at-risk youth as they can relate to their lived experiences. In fact, elder mentors can feel similar emotions of isolation and feel misunderstood by family and community members (Mano, 2007). Consequently, elders need to be used in mentoring more purposefully as their ability to contribute to the development of young people can play a critical role. Unfortunately, these relationships are declining for at-risk youth as they are more likely to have younger grandparents who offer less support in their upbringing (Mano, 2007). Despite the efforts of mentors, young or old, familial or non-familial, mentoring is fraught with many obstacles as it attempts to minimize the challenges at-risk youth must deal with every day.

Eugene L. Moore, Ph.D.

Challenges of Mentoring

Mentoring continues to be a heavily sought after intervention having gained credence both federally and in the private sector. But this increased demand, in turn, increases the need to demonstrate the effectiveness of the services provided. Assessing these programs can be difficult because mentoring operates on two levels — the dyadic relationship between the mentor and mentee and the overall program structure. Thus, it is imperative to assess mentoring based on the interconnected components of the mentoring relationship and the program (Deutsch and Spencer, 2009). Mentoring at-risk youth is not an easy task. For example, in a school setting, it requires extensive training for staff and at a personal level, a high level of commitment (McCluskey, Noller, Lamoureux, & McCluskey, 2004). Despite the research suggesting the positive effects of mentoring, it is important to remember the significant responsibility that comes with mentoring, especially when the results are less optimal. However, it is also important to interrogate the intervention of mentoring beyond simply accepting that it has the potential to deliver positive outcomes. Mentoring is generally understood for forming a connection between a young person and an older adult, but what lacks is in-depth understanding about the nature, quality and the path the mentoring relationship encompasses (Deutsch and Spencer, 2009). It is equally important to be aware that mentoring can have some negative effects on youth and programs must account for this reality to avoid placing the at-risk youth at yet a greater disadvantage.

Negative Effects of Mentoring

In Breaking the Circle of One... (Mullen, Cox, Boettcher, & Adoue, 1997), an author describes her negative mentoring experience as an African-American youngster in kindergarten stating:

> I remember also my persistence in talking. I talked about learning and every wonderful experience of acquiring knowledge. I never disrespected my teacher; in fact, I never said a mean word to or about her. She was a messenger of power. She represented learning, and I wanted every morsel available. My conduct grades were deplorable, while my academic grades were superior. For many children, such an experience could have been traumatic in many nonproductive ways. However, that kindergarten teacher was a negative mentor who attempted to, and succeeded in, silencing the persistence and resilience of my voice, instead of molding it.

Like this instance, there are times when mentorship can have a negative impact. Fortunately, for this inquisitive young girl, she had a multi-level support system that cultivated her thirst for knowledge. Typically, at-risk youth are without a natural support network, so they are heavily reliant on the relationships forged through mentoring — making the need for excellence and quality doubly important.

Cross-aged mentoring, pairing younger children with older adolescents from high school, either in one-on-one relationships or peer groups can prove problematic despite having some positive effects as it typically offers less staff support, contact and direction (Karcher, Herrera, and Hansen, 2010). While mentoring can be effective, we must be cognizant of making sure mentors are equipped with the needed resources to deliver a meaningful experience for the mentee. Recent research is moving away from the broader question whether mentoring works, to more specific questions of how and under what circumstances is it most effective (Pedersen, Woolum, Gagne, and Coleman, 2009). Thus, it is important to fully understand the inner workings of mentoring and make needed adjustments to ensure at-risk youth are receiving the best services possible. In (Mullen, Cox, Boettcher, & Adoue, 1997) the author uses poetry to explain the salient reality of mentoring and the need to embody the collective to gain a greater sense of self and provide a commitment to the future stating, "The circle embodies who I am, what we must become, and where we must go to transform the lives of the future" (p. 4). The poem captures the need for effective mentorship, where effective means a mentee has established a relationship with a mentor that is consistent and produces positive outcomes. At-risk youth are faced with many challenges and a feeling of belonging is one of the many obstacles they endure. Whether an at-risk youth is exposed to school-based mentoring or a community-based intervention, creating a positive relationship for these children is imperative because without positive mentoring, options for failure seem inescapable and success can seem impossible. Stumbo, Blegen, and Lindahl-Lewis (2008) state, "Mentorship programs, however, need to be well planned and designed and have both a comprehensive implementation and evaluation plan in place prior to initiation" (p.45). Wandersman, Clary, Forbush, Weinberger, Coyne, and Duffy (2006) state, "Mentoring programs have the potential to contribute to positive youth development, yet that potential is not always realized" (p. 783). Pryce (2012) offers some opposition to the perceived notion that youth mentoring is a total win-win, but adds a point of contention to the debate stating:

> Although mentoring represents a popular and widespread in-

tervention, the experience of transformation aspired to by the iconic mentoring relationship represents an exceptional level of effort and commitment. In fact, research suggests that many youth mentoring relationships fall short; instead, many have limited positive effects or positive effects that are temporary.

Like almost everything, there will be good and bad. Fortunately, many youth have benefited from the positive effects of mentoring but minimizing the negative outcomes should always remain a goal. Mentoring's familiarity and potential to produce positive outcomes do not remove the obligation to be critical of it as an intervention — further unpacking the consequences of the intervention is still necessary.

Mentee Perspectives

Darling, Bogat, Cavell, Murphy, and Sanchez (2006) state, "At its core, the mentoring movement tries to foster relationships that promote positive developmental trajectories in protégés and, potentially, in mentors as well. Mentoring relationships are shaped by the unique qualities each partner contributes to the dyad" (p. 766). Mentors face many challenges ranging from scheduling to being paired with mentees to whom they do not connect. Liang and Rhodes (2007) state, "To be effective, mentors need to tolerate all kinds of uncertainties, to address ethical dilemmas and disappointments as they arise, and to know whom to turn to for consultation and how to work through uncharted territories" (p. 104). Day (2006) provides an anonymous poem, written by a mentee, espousing the power of mentoring and the appreciation afforded great mentors.

Some people specialize in doing thoughtful deeds,

Before you ask they understand your problems

And your needs.

They help because they want to;

They find that being kind,

And making others happy is the first thing on their mind.

They make this world a better place by practicing the art,

Of reaching out to others

And by giving from the heart.

Mentees often experience disappointments, but have life-changing experiences when they are exposed to positive role models. Anda (2001) offers a personal perspective from a mentee who described a perfect mentor:

A perfect mentor would be someone you could always talk to; someone you could ask them for advice, and they would always give you the best advice. And in the future when you're grown up, you could look back and say 'they really helped me; they've really been there and a great role model.'

Such testimonies prove the natural power of mentoring — an advantageous experience for the mentee and mentor that often also meets the expectation of parents who encouraged the caring adult-youth relationship. But these mentor-mentee relationships for at-risk youth need continuous refinement to maintain their effectiveness.

At the center of the mentoring debate, besides the issues that our youth face, we cannot lose track of the goal to ensure all children are afforded comparable opportunities. Programs must focus on improving the quality of service and the relationships forged through the process. Figuring out what makes an effective relationship may present a challenge, but it is imperative for programs and researchers to address it in order to ensure that we are providing youth with the most favorable experiences to best support their growth, development and overall future (Deutsch and Spencer, 2009). It seems obvious that mentoring will continue to be an intervention for at-risk youth, but overarching the mentoring efforts, there also need to be actions to ameliorate the underlying social ills these youth face. To ensure at-risk youth have great programs, we must continue to recruit and train mentors to serve these vulnerable populations. We must not blame failed mentoring programs or otherwise shift the responsibility, but be unwavering in our commitment to provide mentoring relationships with positivity.

This chapter's discussion of mentoring, its complexities and the populations it serves, reveals that more research must be done to discover ways to strengthen mentor-mentee relationships as society continues to change. Perhaps the goal is lofty, but maybe the term "at-risk" will not be the common descriptor for so many of African-American youth. It was disheartening to learn/confirm through research both how vulnerable these youth are and how minimal the progress has been despite efforts to provide support. Nonetheless, mentoring certainly has some substantial benefits. All mentoring has the potential to enhance young peoples' lives by bolstering their social capital — their knowledge of and contacts with a network of people who are able to help them meet their goals through various activities and interactions. These relationships allow two worlds to be bridged, the advantaged and disadvantaged in hopes that the bridge produces hope and opportunity for at-risk youth (Hamilton, Hamilton, Hirsh, Hughes, King, and Maton, 2006).

Success is not easy even for those who are equipped with abundant resources, but it is hard to imagine the resiliency an at-risk youth must have to overcome some of life's most difficult circumstances. Perhaps bridging the social capital of the affluent or those who have experiences outside of poverty, will provide some needed hope for at-risk youths from single-parent homes or other challenging societal issues. These young people often seek these much needed positive relationships in their lives. Like many single-parents, my mother sensed the gravity of our ascribed circumstance, so instinctively, she encouraged and fostered a welcoming environment for the mentor-mentee relationship — those thirty years of relationships were life-changing and continue to produce positive outcomes. Because the mentor-mentee relationship continues to be a common intervention for school-aged African-Americans, it is imperative for researchers, scholars, policy-makers and all those committed to the betterment of at-risk youth to ensure its programmatic structures are capable of delivering positive, sustainable outcomes.

CHAPTER 3
METHODOLOGICAL APPROACH AND RESEARCH DESIGN

This chapter covers the design used to guide this research study. Data was obtained using interviews of at-risk youth participating in an after-school mentoring program. More specifically, the chapter covers the research methodology including the research setting; the rationale for using interviews; structure sampling and participants; snowball sampling; advantages and disadvantages of snowball sampling, description of participants, equipment usage, qualitative research methods; grounded theory; data collection; data analysis; data reliability and validity; methodological limitations and considerations; and cultural context and understanding. These sections are intended to supply context and clarity for how the study was conducted.

RESEARCH SETTING

In 2013 the Community Youth Center was on the verge of closing and its membership had fallen to under 50 members. Today the center has nearly 500 members and is on target to impact 1,500 children in 2017. On an average day, the center attracts about 160 kids from kindergarten to 18 years of age. The membership fee of $20.00 is waived for those families who cannot afford to pay it. The hours of operation are from 7:30am until 9:00pm. After-school programs for the non-teens run from 2:00pm until 5:00pm and for teenagers, from 4:00pm until 9:00pm. Impressive membership numbers and the more than 12 hours of daily operations of the center are not reflected in staff numbers. Staff turnover is high and replacements are difficult to recruit primarily due to low wages and the transitory nature of the community. In addition, the facility has inadequate capacity to meet the community demand for quality programs. Most of the game equipment, like the pool table, is either outdated or missing key parts to support its functionality. The Community Youth Center is nearly 50 years old. Despite a renovation in the early 90's, it is in need of structural upgrades, as well as funding, to support current and prospective programs. The Community Youth Center is a non-profit whose ability to leverage its offerings is completely contingent upon the generosity of its donors. Although many upgrades are needed, the center still manages to serve the kids. Entering the center shortly after 5:00 p.m. feels like walking into utter chaos. The intercom system is continually blaring when kids' rides arrive. Most kids continue to play and begrudgingly come to the front only after being called multiple times and their parent or authorized adult has expressed his frustration, "I'm ready to go!" As the younger kids leave, teenagers disperse throughout the center to the multipurpose area, the game room, the computer lab, the teen lounge, or upstairs to the gymnasium — by far the most popular gathering place — they love to play basketball. The environment is filled with fun, laughter and occasional banter as the members engage in various supervised activities. The multipurpose room, which serves as a meeting place for all members, is an open space with various floor games like pool, carpet ball, hockey and arcade games.

Rationale for Using Interviews

Interviews were concluded to be the most effective data collection method for the research study. Although there are other notable forms of qualitative methods like focus groups or ethnography, the researcher strongly believes individual, semi-formal interviews allowed room to gather more personalized data and provide a rich dialogue for analysis. Kvale (1996) states, "The knowledge generated by interviews is related to five features of post-modern consideration of knowledge: the conversational, the narrative, the linguistic, the contextual, and the interrelational nature of knowledge" (p. 42). These five themes were incorporated throughout the interview process because they are important elements to how the interview process gains knowledge. In the researcher's experience as a mentee and now mentor, he fully understands the intrinsic value of mentoring stems from the inherent value the mentor-mentee relationship has within itself and for its own sake. (Zimmerman, 2014). As humans we innately try to make sense of our relationships, so we often reflect and rely on stories that represent those lived experiences. The researcher imagines if he talked with his peers from his seventh-grade class, their stories would be different but the variance in the stories should not delegitimize them — it is the importance of understanding how others often experience the same situation differently. These individualized accounts allow us to understand how each mentee is responding to the mentor-mentee relationship and its overall effectiveness or lack thereof.

The research presents the narratives provided by participants involved in the Extend-a-Hand Program, a structured mentoring program for at-risk youth. While it may seem more advantageous to use focus groups, the researcher elected to use individual interviews to increase assurance of the authenticity of the responses. Group settings can greatly affect comfortability to share information, whereas individual semi-formal interviews give the participants more freedom to share their narrative without filtering or the subconscious desire to compete. This environment fostered a safe space for participants to tell their stories without the fear of judgment by their peers or program leaders more likely when using a focus group. The participants were asked 25 questions during the interview session, producing large amounts of information within the projected scope of the project. The data was thoroughly analyzed and presented using the highest level of integrity.

The researcher conducted semi-formal one-on-one interviews with each participant to create an environment that was conducive to rich dialogue. The Community Youth Center has multiple after school programs running concurrently. Most of its programs are voluntary, but the Extend-a-Hand Program is unique because it is based on referrals from school officials, the juvenile court system, or community leaders. This parameter made semi-formal one-on-one interviews more advantageous because this targeted population is highly at-risk and according to staff are less focused and easily distracted in group settings. Furthermore, the researcher did not want to take participants on an emotional journey aimed to bolster the research at the expense of leaving the participants vulnerable and exposed. Interviews allowed participants to engage in casual conversations with the freedom to be open and expressive without feeling overly analyzed by the interviewer. Another possible limitation of a focus group far outweighed that of semi-formal interviews — the researcher could not account for the time it would take to engage in a collective conversation with varying viewpoints often in play simultaneously. In addition, qualitative interviews afforded the researcher flexibility to respond to follow-up questions when appropriate without having to consider multiple viewpoints that would have likely been present in a focus group. So after much consideration, the individual semi-formal interview was selected as the primary form of data collection.

Structure Sampling and Participants

In qualitative research, there are several strategies for selecting potential participants including simple random sampling, systemic sampling, cluster sampling and stratified sampling. Most of these techniques use two approaches — one hinging on the theoretical and the other based on a single case. Theoretical sampling operates under the premise that the ideas about the case, in the beginning are vague and only materialize during the course of the investigation. In contrast, single case techniques have more concrete ideas about the study at the onset allowing for more generalized conclusions for the group who shares the same characteristics (Flick, Kardorff, and Steinke, 2004). After careful analysis and consideration of these techniques, the researcher elected to use snowball sampling. This proved more appropriate based on the potential pool of participants at the research site and the amount of time the researcher could feasibly give to support the study.

Snowball Sampling

Snowball sampling is a readily used method for qualitative research as it can be easily implemented to reach a targeted population, especially when the study is primarily explorative and descriptive. Researchers frequently use snowball sampling because of its ease of application and cost-effectiveness. Conducting a large-scale research study accounting for all members of a population (like census data) is inherently taxing both financially and in the amount of time needed to collect and analyze the data. Frey, Botan, and Kreps (2000) refer to snowball sampling as network sampling. The network incorporates potential participants who they believe have the necessary experience for inclusion in the study. The Extend-a-Hand Program at Prairie Urban is funded by the state. It requires 20-30 participants and according to staff, currently had 22 members (73% male and 27% female). As a result, the sample size was rather small. This made purposive sampling less feasible for participant selection. Thus, snowball sampling was an effective method given the sample size. The researcher interviewed 10 participants (8 males and 2 females) — this group was statistically diverse in age and gender, based on the overall population of the program. Most participants self-identify as African-American and come from households with incomes at or below state poverty indicators.

In general, snowball sampling proves to have both advantages and disadvantages — these are explained later to ensure transparency. It can be applied both as an informal and formal methodology (Hendricks, Blanken and Adriaans, 1992). Snowball sampling is also called nominated sampling because it elicits the support of participants to nominate others to participate in the study (Brink and Wood, 1989). This process assumes there is a bond or connection between the initial participant/informant and the same target population allowing a series of nominations to be provided (Berg, 1988). The researcher connected with new participants by introducing themselves to the prospective informant or the previous participant reached out to his or her suggested participant. Both sampling processes have fluidity and unlike other methods, has a better chance of connecting with potential informants. The process of finding participants can be laborious, but snowball sampling has proven effective when the researcher adheres to the potential limitations the method presents. The participants of the Extend-a-Hand Program were more than willing to refer future participants, coupled with staff informant suggestions.

Disadvantages and Advantages of Snowball Sampling

Some of the known disadvantages to snowball sampling include: 1) the population from which the pool of participants is selected can present a level of bias that could negatively impact the findings 2) the snowball sampling method can be limiting for the researcher as he is reliant on the current participant to generate future informants 3) there is no way to determine the size and depth of the total population 4) it is impossible to determine if the sample population is a true indication of the target population and 5) it fails to incorporate random selection. For example, if the informant has ill intent, he could suggest an informant that will align with his views thus permanently introducing bias. Also, data collection can be delayed because the researcher lacks control of the sampling method. To mitigate these situations, the researcher asked the participants to refer individuals based on certain criteria like age and gender to guard against the potential bias of just referring individuals who may share similar viewpoints of the recommender. Providing clear instructions about what characteristics are sought can reduce the inherent biases snowball sampling can produce (King and Horrocks, 2010). Given that the total target population of the study is large in scope, the snowball sampling method cannot reasonably reflect the overall population. It is equally important to note, however, that the snowball sampling method contradicts many of the assumptions and/or benefits of random selection.

The advantages of snowball sampling are as follows: 1) it allows the researcher to access hidden populations 2) provides the flexibility of locating people of a specific population and 3) it is cost-effective. When a researcher enters a research site his access to hidden populations can be limited, even when he extends financial resources like offering gift cards or monetary incentives. In the conduct of research, one of the primary goals is ensuring a strategic methodological approach to locate the targeted population — this is an effective advantage of snowball sampling. Conducting research can be costly, irrespective of the scope of the study. Surveying large populations (similar to the U.S. Census) can produce an astronomical price tag, thus making snowball sampling a cost-effective alternative. The Extend-a-Hand Program Coordinator provided full access to all participants' files which included their school grades, infractions and case notes. In addition, the Program Coordinator provided a brief overview of her personal interactions with each participant and why each was referred to the program. The informational support of the Program Coordinator and her ability to help the researcher connect with respondents allowed snowball sampling to be easily incorporated.

Description of Participants

The participants in this study were at-risk African-American teenagers aged 13-18 years of age, who are members of the Community Youth Center and more specifically, actively participating in the Extend-a-Hand Program. Pseudonyms were used to protect the identity of the participants and staff of the Community Youth Center. Members of the staff closely linked to the program were interviewed to glean a clear understanding of how they viewed the mentor-mentee relationship. The researcher employed snowball sampling to select participants who were capable of providing robust data that could be generalized to the larger population. The researcher accounted for those participants who chose not to participate for various reasons, whether they were clearly stated or unknown, to avoid unintentionally creating inherent obstacles in the study.

Gaining accessibility is critical to ensure the researcher has the ability to select participants for the study (Flick, 2004). The study relied heavily on the integrity, comfortability, honesty, and validity of the participant to provide meaningful, reliable information. Thus, staff assisted in establishing trust with the participants; then the researcher using the interview questions as a guide, allowed the participant to lead the dialogue in an organic and unanticipated direction. In addition, because the researcher used snowball sampling, it was equally important the participant recommended or referred potential participants who adhered to the guidelines set forth by the research study. The participants served as key informants based on their expert knowledge and familiarity of the Extend-a-Hand Program, the programmatic structure of the Community Youth Center, the community demographics, historical context and their individual experiences. When a participant or informant provides critical context and content, it adds relevant value to the overall study (Fraenkel & Wallen, 2011).

Finally, all participants are members of the Community Youth Center. As such, a requirement of their membership is consenting to participate in potential research studies approved by the center. In addition to the center's consent form, the researcher provided them with another, explaining the parameters of the study and requesting their voluntary consent. As mentioned earlier, each member is required under the terms of the membership agreement to participate in research studies approved by the Community Youth Center. Additionally, to further protect the interest of the University of Illinois at Urbana-Champaign, the researcher and the research subjects gained an approved consent form through the Institutional Review Board (IRB).

Equipment Usage

The researcher used a digital voice recording device to audiotape conversations among participants and when conducting one-on-one interviews. Although the recording device was on throughout the duration of the interview, the researcher took detailed notes of the dialogue to supplement the recording. In addition to using the voice recorder, the researcher also used a smartphone to simultaneously record the conversation to serve as a backup in the event of technical difficulties with the digital recorder. The smartphone was set to restrict incoming alerts, texts, or calls to prevent any interruptions to the recording. During the one-on-one interviews, the participants also wore external microphones to ensure the recorder could clearly pick up the respondents' answers and/or utterances to the questions. The recording devices were plugged into an external power source to ensure the devices were not reliant on their internal battery mechanisms. All information retrieved from the voice recording devices was transcribed and coded to protect the anonymity of the research subjects. The interviews were conducted in the staff office, where members are not allowed unless accompanied by a staff member. The Program Coordinator assured the researcher that the staff office was the best location to conduct the interviews without disruptions. This, in fact, proved to be true.

Qualitative Research Interview Methods

The researcher conducted a qualitative study incorporating grounded theory. Grounded theory is not predicated on preconceived theory nor does it function as a priori theory, but is established using data methodically retrieved during the course of research inquiry (Glasser &Strauss, 1967). Thus, grounded theory postulates the information gained during the research process and informs the theory that the data analysis renders. The researcher's prior experiences with mentoring programs influenced him by generating his personal curiosity, thus making grounded theory a feasible method to apply to the study. The study has greatly informed the researcher's understanding of the mentor-mentee relationship. Hence, through the acquired personalized accounts on how the research subjects define value and understand mentoring in general based on their past and present experiences, the study produced a deeper knowledge of the Extend-a-Hand Program.

Qualitative research is a widely used form of research in which the researcher plays a pivotal role in collecting and interpreting data, thus representing the dichotomous relationship between the researcher and participants (Corbin & Strauss, 2015). There are many approaches and variations to qualitative research, and the researcher employed the theoretical framework he believed was most appropriate for his research design. These variations and approaches inherently give room to different modes of conceptualization used to describe and explain the research findings (Glaser & Strauss, 1967). The researcher received a more robust understanding of what happens during the after-school Extend-a-Hand Program using qualitative research methods — incorporating his inherent curiosity about mentoring and its effectiveness or lack thereof. These methods account for how we as humans epistemologically approach knowledge and debate its truth and limits. Qualitative research does not use mathematical procedures or other forms that incorporate quantification. In fact, it refers to research that has varied interests such as persons' lived experiences, feelings, emotions, cultural and social contexts. These experiences are largely understood by the researcher using interpretive methods based on interviews or observations (Strauss & Corbin, 1998). Thus, the feelings and lived experiences of mentees would be difficult to understand using quantitative methods. Given these considerations, the researcher believed qualitative research provided the best opportunity to understand the phenomena mentees experienced. Moreover, grounded theory helped to develop a theoretical interpretation of what is happening during the Extend-a-Hand Program from the perspective of the participants.

Grounded Theory

Grounded theory operates with the understanding the researcher is on a journey to discover or generate a theory derived from the systematic collection of data guided by implicit standards (Glaser & Strauss, 1967). As a result, grounded theory creates room for contextual introspection rather than just a description of what is occurring within the research setting. The fluid nature of grounded theory produces both substantive and formal theories — substantive theories serve as the springboards to develop a grounded formal theory (Glaser & Strauss, 1967). The researcher was extremely intrigued by the mentor-mentee relationship, and grounded theory provided the flexibility for the research findings to inform and/or shape how the data was analyzed. Grounded theory is well known for incorporating interviews and observations as methods for data collection.

In conjunction with grounded theory, the researcher incorporated the symbolic interactionist perspective which is generally guided by these three principles: 1) humans respond to things based on their predetermined ideas and meanings they have for them; 2) meanings are derived from social interaction and 3) social action occurs by piecing together the individual elements of action (Boundless, 2016). The primary function/rationale for applying symbolic interaction to this study is to provide credence between the dichotomous relationship between the researcher and his or her participants. It would be irrational to assume the researcher's prior experience as a mentee and his professional experience as a mentor did not influence how he interpreted the data. Hence, symbolic interactions make the relationship between the researcher and participant more natural and less awkward. The researcher used his personal knowledge of mentoring to contextualize the data to bring a clear understanding of the findings. Grounded theory implicitly attempts through the analysis of data to develop a theoretical interpretation of what is happening both visually and through active listening (Kvale, 1996). Another major benefit of grounded theory is it gives the researcher flexibility to begin research from a point of interest, but not without adhering to the theoretical framework used to conduct data collection (Dey, 1999). The participants provided authentic accounts of their lived experiences related to their mentor-mentee relationships. As mentioned earlier in the chapter, the participants have been referred to the Extend-a-Hand Program by their school, probationary officer, or community member as a corrective measure to improve their academic and social standing. During the interviews and observations, the participants expressed numerous infractions within the school system ranging from fighting and other behavioral indiscretions.

Data Collection

Throughout the entire process of data collection, it was essential the researcher maintained the highest level of integrity and sensitivity to all the information retrieved during the process. The researcher in no way wanted to trivialize, marginalize, or discredit any thoughts and comments received during the interview process. In an effort to maintain this standard, the digital audio recording was meticulously transcribed, coded and will be securely stored for at least one year after the conduct of the study to ensure authenticity and that the conceptual framework was adequately applied.

At the onset of the interview process, it was imperative to give forethought for how the researcher would start and finish the interviews. How the process starts can have either positive or negative effects as it relates to building rapport. Questions should be relatively non-threatening and somewhat simple in scope which could include more descriptive information (King & Horrocks, 2010). The Program Coordinator informed all 22 Extend-a-Hand Program participants of the researcher's role. In addition to receiving the coordinator's support, the researcher spent the first month simply observing the participants. During the observation, the researcher took detailed field notes and used coding to develop possible themes. The result of the researcher's observations and interviews was a detailed account of how participants understood their experience within the Extend-a-Hand Program. Triangulation occurred as the researcher collected data from interviews and observations, coded the findings, and created themes. The researcher's association with higher education was a barrier at first, according to staff members, because of the contentious relationship between the community and institutions of higher education. The researcher overcame this barrier by explaining his at-risk upbringing and past membership in an organization similar to the Community Youth Center.

Data Analysis

According to Kvale (1996), "Analysis is not an isolated stage but permeates an entire interview inquiry" (p. 205). The permeation of which Kvale speaks ranges from coding to the categorizing of data. Coding allows the researcher to create reoccurring themes to further analyze data.

Throughout the data collection, the researcher took detailed field notes and jottings to supplement the audio recordings. To stay engrossed in the discussion, the researcher continually took notes during the interview sessions and reviewed the audio recording for additional reflection. Once the information was accurately coded, the recurring themes were organized to reflect the developed categories. In a real sense each interview, interaction, and occurrence informed the proceeding interview, interaction, and occurrence. For example, if a participant revealed they had a learning disability, strained relationship with a family member, or a custodial parent who is incarcerated, the researcher expressed interest in knowing how prior participants have similar or varied experiences. Therefore, the concurrent data analysis becomes critical to further develop theory.

Open coding is the process by which the researcher generates initial concepts derived from the data. Axial coding provides the necessary structure to create and correlate similar themes in a coding paradigm. Selective or substantive coding occurs after primary concepts, themes and categories have been identified through data analysis (Corbin & Strauss, 1990). The researcher incorporated open, axial and selective coding during the analysis process as the Program Coordinator had informed the researcher that although the participants have similar backgrounds, how similar experiences manifested in their lives had some significant variance. For example, one participant coming from a broken home may exhibit aggression while another experiences feelings of isolation. Having these various options when coding data was critical in ensuring the appropriate themes were derived.

Eugene L. Moore, Ph.D.

Data Reliability and Validity

One of the major goals of conducting qualitative research is to demonstrate reliability. The researcher cross-checked the findings extrapolated from the data set to determine validity. The audio recordings, transcriptions, coded field notes and other jottings were memo and peer verified to ensure their accuracy. For example, while transcribing audio recordings the researcher utilized a peer to confirm they were hearing the correct utterances and recording the data accurately. The field notes and memos allowed the researcher to compare the recordings and even add some contextual description that was expressed nonverbally. Thus, the findings proved to be reliable and accurate as is warranted when conducting a qualitative study. King and Horrocks (2010) state, "reliability is concerned with how accurately any variable is measured, while validity is concerned with determining whether a particular form of measurement actually measures the variable it claims to" (p. 158). It seems reliability serves as a necessary prerequisite to validity. For example, if the researcher was incapable of gaining a consistent level of observation it becomes more probable the findings would reflect that inconsistency. Similarly, validity is concerned with ensuring the credibility and/or truthfulness of the research findings. Thus, the primary role of the researcher is to present plausible and credible evidence that was garnered from the data collection process and analysis (Flick, 2004). Potential threats to validity are reactivity, researcher and respondent bias (Padgett, 2008). Reactivity occurs when the presence of the researcher causes the subject to alter their behavior. For example, when the researcher first entered the Community Youth Center it was immediately clear he was an outsider. Until he gained trust some respondents did not behave at their level of normalcy. In fact, there were constant whispers among the teens trying to figure out the new face at the Community Youth Center.

As mentioned earlier the researcher has a long-standing experience with mentoring. If he had not been cognizant of his own biases, it would have created a greater probability of distorting the findings. Given the respondents former and current experience with mentoring their biases can greatly hinder the findings. Kvale (1996) states, "Bias may be on the side of the interviewee or of the interviewer" (p. 286). The researcher has to be aware of the unintentional and even unacknowledged bias he or his respondents possess. Do the researcher's reflections on his past experience as a mentee totally void his current knowledge, or is he simply recalling the events based on how he felt at that time? In fact, the researcher could have selective memory and choose to recall what he considers important. All of these realities, if not addressed and adequately remedied, would threaten the reliability and validity of the study.

LIMITATIONS OF METHODOLOGY

In qualitative research no matter how well the study is designed it will inherently present some limitations — time, availability, financial resources, and limited access to potential subjects. Even the snowball sampling to obtain respondents posed a limitation because this method inherently restricts access to all viable participants. Even though the current interviewees suggest or refer who they believe would be valuable participants in the study, it becomes highly probable all viable participants will not be included. Limited funding and time constraints of both the program itself and the researcher's personal obligations limited those individuals they would feasibly be capable of interviewing. The researcher was limited by his outsider status. Furthermore, attempting to draw upon his personal experiences was not enough to allow the researcher to gain insight into some of the participants' experiences. Fortunately, the Program Coordinator had an overall knowledge of each participant, so he was able to provide a holistic view into the individualized narrative of each teen participating in the Extend-a-Hand Program. This included critical, detailed information about family background, school behavior, and infractions of the law.

Methodological Considerations

While a researcher reviews and analyzes data, missed opportunities in the questioning process can become abundantly clear. Most researchers probably acknowledge the need to ask another question or to further examine a reoccurring theme with greater intensity. Therefore, the researcher informed each participant during the initial interview of the possibility the dialogue could be extended beyond the predetermined questions. Intentionality and transparency are important in the researcher's approach to facilitate asking more probing follow-up questions, if necessary, after the initial interview.

In addition to these methodological considerations, it would be somewhat irresponsible to not acknowledge human error. Even the most revered researchers and academic scholars openly admit there are missed opportunities due to human errors. Beyond normal human error, it is equally probable during the collection process that there will be other misunderstandings and misinterpretations that create some missteps that blur the intended message of the interviewee. It is important to consider the age and varied level of educational astuteness the participants exhibited as it could possibly impede the study if not properly addressed. For example, a 14-year-old participant might not understand the level of questioning, so questions may require rewording to garner understanding. Additionally, the level of experience of a younger participant might be far less than an older participant who has potentially had more mentor-mentee relationships. The researcher's awareness of these potential occurrences helped hone his interpretation as he conducted the research study.

Cultural Context and Cultural Understanding

Potential issues could have arisen if the cultural context and understandings informing this study were not addressed. The Community Youth Center is situated in a micro-urban community with a population of approximately 232,000 according to the 2010 US Census. This includes a transient college-student population from the local university. As mentioned earlier members of the center are required to consent to participate in approved research studies. It was necessary to consider that participants could demonstrate a preconceived mistrust of researchers because of their frequency at the center, but this was certainly not the case. The researcher engaged with the participants by playing basketball, pool and carpet ball — thus allowing the researcher to gain rapport and trust. The center is in a predominately African-American community with high concentrations of crime and poverty. Based on crime reports from Neighborhood Scouts this micro-urban site has a higher crime rate than the state with Prairie Urban at 6.8% and the state at 3.8% respectively. It has the third highest poverty rate in the state at 23.4% according to Social Impact Research Center. Researchers, using the Community Youth Center as their research venue, are usually more affluent than their potential subjects and if not, are still seen by center members as representing the affluence of the neighboring university. The researcher would not have gained the trust of the participants had he not appeared trustworthy and authentic irrespective of shared experiences, being African-American and having had mentor-mentee relationships. The academic language used in scholarly journals, university classrooms and national conferences would have no value in the setting of the Community Youth Center. Consequently, the researcher created an environment void of complicated rhetoric so that subjects could freely express themselves without feeling their language was inferior or inadequate compared to that of the researcher.

Qualitative research can be convoluted. To declutter the process the researcher provided a detailed account of how the study was conducted. The researcher began the opening chapter discussing the purpose and rationale of the study, a key component to qualitative research because it identifies how the study contributes to the field of scholarly research. Once the researcher established the rationale and purpose of the study, he provided the central questions used to guide the research coupled with the interview questions the researcher asked the research participants. Also covered and equally important was how the researcher sampled the teen population to find viable participants. Finally, by explaining the methods, data collection and analysis, researcher bias and methodological limitations and considerations, the reader has the full scope of the conduct of the study. The researcher believes the study produces a greater understanding of the social phenomenon that occurs at the Community Youth Center during the Extend-a-Hand Program and ultimately contributes another facet to the scholarship of mentoring as it relates to the mentor-mentee relationship.

Chapter 4
Research Findings

This chapter will walk through the lives of 10 African-American at-risk teens participating in the Extend-a-Hand Program during the fall of 2016. Their lives are far more dynamic than some might assume. During a four-month period, the researcher observed the participants, while they were engaged in structured activities and social interaction, 2-3 times per week for a minimum of one hour. Through the process of merging the teens' responses to the 25 interview questions, the researcher's observations and the Program Coordinator's detailed report of each participant, the lives of these teens unfolded. We will begin the chapter discovering the narratives of twins, Jalen and Justin, siblings Marion and Marshauna, Shaundrel, Marcus, Terrell, Cortez, Jason, and Destiny. The chapter concludes with the 12 interview questions posed to staff that helped the researcher frame their unique understandings of mentoring and how it plays out at the Community Youth Center. The table below provides a snapshot of each teen participant, including their names, ages, grade level, and the reason for being referred to the Extend-a-Hand Program.

Table 1: *Participant Profiles*

Name	Age	Grade	Reason for Referral
Jalen	14	Freshman	Extremely Low-income
Justin	14	Freshman	Extremely Low-income
Marion	17	Junior	Poor Academics, Behavior and Family Dysfunction
Marshauna	13	8th grade	Family Dysfunction
Shaundrel	18	Senior	Poor Academics
Marcus	17	Junior	Criminal Infraction
Terrell	15	Freshman	Criminal Infraction
Cortez	16	Sophomore	Family Dysfunction and Behavior
Jason	15	Freshman	Criminal Infraction
Destiny	14	8th grade	Family Dysfunction

INTRODUCING JALEN AND JUSTIN-BOTH 14 YEARS OLD

Jalen and Justin, 14-year-old fraternal twins, have attended the Community Youth Center for a long period of time. The boys have starkly different personalities in part because Jalen is far more mature. Despite their differences, they both exude a kind, respectful and gentle nature when dealing with adults. The Program Coordinator said about the twins:

> Jalen is very mature, very much mature. Justin is the one that we struggle and work one-on-one with a lot because he struggles academically and just with behavior, peer pressure, a lot of that. But Jalen is extremely mature – and it's actually shocking how much more mature he is than Justin and they're twins. It's just like they're on two different playing fields.

Their differences in personality and interactions with their peers are evident at school. Jalen does exceptionally well in his academics, whereas Justin struggles — but his difficulties never manifest into disrespectful behavior to his teachers or school personnel. Although both are mostly respectful while at the Community Youth Center, they are both occasionally redirected for using foul language. Most teens at the center engage in profanity, but the twins' language differs from that of the others because it is never intended to harm or offend anyone. Their primary risk factor is their extremely low-income status. The Program Coordinator provided insight into why they were referred to the Extend-a-Hand Program:

> They have very, very low-income. I know because we've had donors donate actual clothes to them in the past because their income is so low, the clothes and shoes and stuff like that. They live with their grandma now because their mom passed away, I think about three years ago. Their mom passed away and she was their primary caregiver. So now they live with their grandma and their uncle kind of helps out too. But, yeah, she does a lot for them. I mean I don't have a lot of parent involvement; I've met their grandma like twice and it's only because she's older so she can't really get out the car. It's hard for her to sign papers because she's really old. So they don't have the mentorship. A lot of the love and the fun and all that stuff, they get that here because they just don't have the relationship when they're at home because they stay with their grandma and she can only do so much.

Jalen and Justin are truly good kids, but through no fault of their own find themselves trying to navigate a world with little or no resources. The resilience they exhibit makes their narratives compelling. Oddly enough, the twins see themselves as quite different from each other, despite having endured the same traumatic experiences of losing a parent and having an absent father — so naturally, they communicate the effects of those events differently.

During the early stages of the observation period, Jalen and Justin approached the researcher — who was sitting in a distant corner of the multipurpose room and while still wearing his long winter coat, frantically taking notes — and introduced themselves. Jalen said, "Hello sir" and Justin said, "Hello sir. What you doing?" This was a particularly comforting moment for the researcher, who was by now accustomed to stares from the participants, and being frequently interrupted with mutters, "Who's that?" After weeks of observations, it was time to begin the interview portion of the research study. The first interview was with Justin.

THE INTERVIEW

When asked about his upbringing Justin stated:

> I grew up in a bad neighborhood, but I grew up with my grandma and my mother. But my mom-well, I have a twin brother, too. When me and my twin were 11, our mom died, so we stayed with our grandma.

Justin was eager to answer the questions and talked about the violence of his neighborhood saying, "A quiet neighborhood, kind of. But, then again, more street violence and stuff like that or something." Justin has had a mentor since he was in the fourth or fifth grade when he joined Big Brothers Big Sisters (BBBS). He believes a mentor has the capacity to teach him how to be a man. He started coming to the Community Youth Center when he was in the seventh grade because he felt it was a great place to do homework, get out of the house and have fun after-school. At the Community Youth Center, he is a part of Extend-a-

Hand, Sports Alliance and he leisurely plays basketball, but not nearly as frequently as other participants. He believes a good mentor will serve as a positive role model and is someone who is considered a great person. As far as a bad mentor he was more descriptive stating:

> Someone who cusses all the time, who is someone acts like – who cusses all the time, who's such a bad influence, and has a bad reputation.

He did not think a mentor's gender is not a determining factor in forming a meaningful bond with a mentee; but when asked if he'd be comfortable to talk about sex with a female mentor, he bashfully said, "Kinda" and eventually concluded he'd prefer a male mentor. When asked about the Extend-a-Hand Program, he stated it was a good program but all participants do not get a chance to fully participate. After further questioning, the researcher learned that he was referring to kids in the community — which is true because the Extend-a-Hand Program is based on referrals. When asked about his understanding of the term "at-risk" and how it makes him feel he stated:

> At-risk to me means if you're – say you have something like your job is at-risk or something. It's kinda abandoning. Like I did something.

His short-term goals are to improve his grades and get a job. When he gets older he wants to become an Emergency Medical Technician and finish college. He values mentoring and believes it can have positive results:

> I think it's very important to have a mentor. Someone just to – if you're going through something, they could probably help you with a problem or something. Or just someone to talk to.

I think it's very important.

According to Justin, mentors are not like family members but they have the capacity to help you navigate through tough situations. He is comfortable sharing information about his personal life with his mentor. When asked how he felt his mentor could relate to his upbringing, he said he could not because he is Caucasian and does not know what it means to grow up in a black neighborhood. He also could not understand what it means to lose a parent. Justin initially expressed that race, ethnicity, and gender would not have a great effect on the mentor-mentee relationship, but similar to his response about gender, he later qualified his response about race and decided that race may play a factor depending on the subject being discussed. As the interview ended, we discussed whether he thought the neighborhood surrounding the Community Youth Center was safe and how the center helped reduce crime, violence and dangerous activity. Justin expressed that the community was safe but if he were not attending the center, he would likely get into trouble hanging out in the streets. He feels comfortable inviting his mentor to his home and equally comfortable visiting his mentor's home, which he has done several times. He cannot recall any disappointments he has had with his mentor, but his best experience was attending a college basketball game. He also believes his mentor has the capacity to help him escape the realities of his circumstances by teaching him things he needs to know about life. We concluded the interview with him expressing who he considered the most inspiring person in his life:

> My grandma has inspired me a lot because she always teaches me not to steal. She tells me not to do things. She tells me do my best every day.

The Interview

Jalen says he has been brought up to respect elders and believes his community is pretty good because it is small and everyone knows each other. His definition of mentoring is "someone who is going to help me and guide me in the right direction." His previous experience with mentoring was when he was in fifth grade and participated in the BBBS program. When asked about how he felt about having a mentor he stated:

> My mom, she felt that I needed somebody to help me, instead of being on the streets and like that. I guess it was kind of a mystery finding out who it was gonna be. That's why I signed up.

He has been coming to the Community Youth Center for three years and states why he comes:

> It's the greatest place to be. It helps you with homework. There's a lot of activities you can be in. It basically just give you the opportunity, you know what I'm saying? The center, it helps you out with scholarships and like that.

Jalen is involved in several activities at the Community Youth Center including the Extend-a-Hand Program, the basketball team, and biking. He believes a good mentor is someone that connects with the mentee, gets to know him, and helps him when needed by teaching him the steps he took to become successful. Conversely, he believes a bad mentor is someone who doesn't connect with the mentee and rarely sees him. He believes the mentor does not need to be the same race, ethnicity or gender and expressed he would be comfortable discussing sensitive topics like sex with a female mentor. He believes the Extend-a-Hand Program is good, but he hasn't really participated in any activities outside the center except to go skating. When asked what he feels when he hears the term "at-risk" he stated, "In harm or you're in danger." His short-term goals are to achieve good grades but basically just do well in school. He wants to graduate from high school and go to a community college. When asked how he valued mentor relationships, he stated:

> I think it's a wonderful idea, having someone that can guide you in a way that no one else could. A mentor is a great opportunity to learn something and also you can have a friend to be there for you.

He believes mentor-mentee relationship has both similarities and differences compared to family. Similarly, family and mentors both must establish trust and they can always be there for you. But the difference is the mentor is a stranger, so he has to earn the trust. Jalen expressed being uncomfortable sharing his innermost thoughts with his mentor but he would disclose things like how he was doing in school. Jalen feels that it is difficult for mentors to understand his circumstances — they do not have the ability to walk in his shoes. He feels the neighborhood in close proximity to the Community Youth Center is safe because it is near a police station. When asked if he thought the Community Youth Center could reduce crime, he quickly said yes, stating, "If it wasn't for the center, people would be outside, you know what I'm saying, gangbang." He is comfortable inviting his mentor to his home and watched a game with his mentor and his brother when he visited his home. The most positive times he has with his mentor are when the mentor visits him at school and takes him to lunch, and when they go to the movies. He has not been disappointed by his mentor — their relationship is positive. He believes his mentor has the capacity to help him escape his circumstances by providing resources and guidance. We concluded the interview with him talking about who he considered the most inspiring person in his life:

It would have to be my grandma. My grandma and my mom. Those two that raised me best. No male in the house, so it's up to them. It wasn't too bad because I have two wonderful women who guide me in the right direction. My uncle, he's stepped up and he tries to teach manhood.

Introducing Marion-17 and Marshauna-13

Marion and Marshauna are siblings and long-term members of the Community Youth Center, where their mother coincidentally is a staff member. Marion struggles academically but his grades often fluctuate due to a lack of effort. The Program Coordinator had said this about Marion:

> So Marion is very strongly influenced by his peers, I'll say that. He is very strongly influenced. I think if he hung around better peers, he had a better peer circle, he'll do well. But he likes hanging around kids and try to be tough. And he's already stated to me, "I'm not tough. That's not me." I've already had that conversation with him about that. But, yeah, as far as his risk factors he struggles a lot academically. He doesn't have an IEP [Individualized Education Program], though, but he does struggle a lot. We actually were trying to get him in an alternative school program, but we were not able to because you have to be referred there so we weren't able to get him in there. Just to see if a different learning environment will help him better academically.

In addition to his struggles in school, he has a tense relationship with his mother and is often openly disrespectful. On several occasions, the researcher witnessed Marion screaming at his mother and one instance he even pushed her — but immediately changed his demeanor when she responded authoritatively. Their relationship seems strained but Marion expressed love for his mother on her birthday and told the researcher she was in the hospital due to complications of a long-term blood disorder. His ex-girlfriend, also a member of the Extend-a-Hand Program, was frequently pushed by and talked poorly to by Marion; even though he was continually reprimanded by his mother and several center staff. In contrast to his poor relationship with his mother and ex-girlfriend, he has a good relationship with his father who lives outside the home. He visits his dad mostly on the weekends but talks to him frequently. However, despite their connection, his childhood memories of his father are laced with violence and disappointment. The Program Coordinator provided some context about their tumultuous relationship:

> And a little background about that, a lot of his trauma coming in, and he even told me that he tried counseling and stuff. He and his dad and his mom had a really abusive relationship when they were together and he witnessed a lot of that and he actually tried to intervene as the oldest brother. So that's a lot of trauma that he was dealing with and he went to counseling for that because he saw a lot of that trauma. So now he feels like he has to be like this big, ultimate brother that does everything for his little sister Marshauna and for his mom. So I witnessed a lot of that with Marion, just him feeling like he needs to be the protector and being tough, but he know that's really not necessarily his role. That's just his family dysfunction.

He has had no entanglements with juvenile justice but has frequent suspensions from school because he succumbs to pressure from his peers and gets into huge brawls. Ironically, he does better at the Community Youth Center — the environment is better and he sees it as fun. Also according to the Program Coordinator, his mother enables him by allowing him to act out in school.

Marion's sister, Marshauna, is 13 years old and like her brother has a close relationship with their father. Her dad often brings her lunch to school — by all accounts, she is a daddy's girl. According to the Program Coordinator, their mother seems to display some resentment because of the children's desire to spend lots of time with their father. She has heard the mother say, "So you going to your daddy's house again? No, you need to stay home and do your homework!" The Coordinator contends the family dysfunction is mostly represented with the parents and not necessarily with the children. The mother refers to their father as, "the sperm donor" and refers to him as such when the children visit him. Another interesting family dynamic is the father has a daughter from a previous relationship who also attends the Community Youth Center. Ironically she and Marshauna are best friends despite the tension between Marshauna's mother and their father.

The Interview

Marion was open during his interview and confirmed a lot of the information provided by the Program Coordinator. When asked about his upbringing he stated:

> I grew up in a home where there's a lot of abuse. My mom got abused a lot. It was just me, my mom, and my baby sister. Well, I was young, so I really couldn't do nothing about it. So I felt like it was my fault.

When asked about conditions where he currently lives, he initially stated they were okay but needed some improvements. But when further probed, he stated:

> All the shooting and crimes they can stop it. People could get off the streets if they really tried. If they had somebody in their life that could push them to the right success.

He believes a mentor is someone who cares about you, displays love towards you, and most importantly is willing to help you if needed. When asked about his first time having a mentor he stated:

> First introduced to mentoring, I think it was when I was 14. Mr. Young (Program Director of the Community Youth Center) had got me a mentor, and it was pretty nice. Me and my mentor we got a lot in common, and it was nice to see that I wasn't the only one that had come from a bad family.

Marion has been coming to the center for more than 10 years. He will miss some days if he is working but still comes frequently. He is involved in the Extend-a-Hand Program and a member of the basketball team. When asked why he comes to the center, he stated:

> I guess because I don't want to be on the streets like most people, and I want my mom to care for me. And I know there are people here that I can trust because they helped me get my first job here. So they helped me with that, and then the job that I have now they helped me get it too because, like, the guy that used to work here his wife, I mean, his girlfriend's dad owns the place where I work at. So he helped me get the job.

When asked what he considered good mentoring he stated:

> Where a mentor checks up on you almost every two weeks and just talks to you and see how you're doing in school and how life is going and if you need help doing anything or need help getting anything.

Conversely, when asked who he would consider a bad mentor he stated:

> Where you don't talk to your mentor at all, and you just only see him, like, probably once a year or something like that.

He believes the race, ethnicity, and gender are important. He believes a female mentor would have a more difficult time to show him how to live in the world and compares this example to his contentious relationship with his mother. He likes the Extend-a-Hand Program because of the vast activities the program features. He believes the term "at-risk" demonstrates someone who is in trouble and is in desperate need of help — this creates some anxiety for the person who is in trouble. His short-term goal, to graduate from high school, will require him to improve his grades. His long-term goals are to attend Tuskegee University in Alabama and become an automotive engineer with hopes of building his own car. He values mentoring relationships stating:

> Because, like, some people they don't have either a father figure or a female figure in their life, so they get a mentor so they can feel better and have somebody that they know that can care for them.

He believes mentor-mentee relationships are similar to that of family members given the closeness of the relationship. He is comfortable sharing his innermost thoughts and feelings with his mentor because he is capable of listening and would not share his thoughts with others. He believes his mentor relates to his upbringing because they are similar. This may possibly have a huge effect on his decisions. He thinks the neighborhood around the center is relatively safe depending on the day of the week. For example, weekends are more violent because more people are on the streets doing crazy things. He believes the center plays an integral role in reducing violence because it helps keep kids off the streets. He is comfortable inviting his mentor to his home and recalled his visit for Thanksgiving two years ago. And he has visited his mentor's home. The most positive experience with his mentor was when his mentor helped him calm his anger and deal with a disappointment when he was going through a difficult time with his dad. He has had no disappointments relating to the irrelationship and believes his mentor has the capacity to help him escape the realities of his circumstances stating:

> By pushing me to do the right things and pushing me to do everything the right way so that I won't be, like, other people that's done failed already.

To conclude the interview he provided an example of who he believed has inspired him:

> There's a lot of people that I could say, but, like, the main one is – I have to go with Mr. Young because he's a great influence person. He influenced me on a lot of things, and he helped me get my very first mentor that I know that they cared about me and that would be there for me and work things out with me.

The Interview

Marshauna was raised to treat people how she wants to be treated — to respect others. She informed the researcher she has lived in a single-parent home since her parents divorced when she was younger. She contends the community where she lives is good or bad, largely contingent upon where one hangs out. She said, "It depends on who you hang out with. If you hang out with the wrong people then you can get into too much drama." She believes mentoring is getting help from others and forming a relationship of mutual respect. She recalls being in the BBBS program but has no memory of the experience other than she had a mentor. She did recall her first mentoring experience through the IMP (In focus Mentoring Program). She said it had lots of fun activities and helped students with homework. She has been coming to the Community Youth Center since kindergarten and enjoys her time at the center because she is able to participate in fun activities with her friends and complete her homework. She is involved in several activities at the Community Youth Center like Operation Care, Hairstyle and the Extend-a-Hand Program. She believes what makes a good mentor-mentee relationship is the ability to share information, have mutual respect and the ability to learn new things. Conversely, a bad mentor is some who exposes the mentee's personal information and offers little to no help. For the most part, she does not have a preference about the race, ethnicity or gender of her mentor but believes certain sensitive topics like sex or female issues are best shared with a mentor of the same gender. She likes the Extend-a-Hand Program because it exposes her to new opportunities like college trips. When asked about the term "at-risk" and how being defined as such would make her feel, she stated she did not know what it meant. The researcher explained the definition as someone who has high-risk factors like low-income, substance abuse, single-parent homes and communities with high drop rates. Once she understood the term and its implications she stated, "I would feel offended." Her short-term goal is to get her grades up by receiving mostly A's and B's in her classes. Her long-term goals are to complete high school and go to college. She believes the mentor-mentee relationship is important because it provides someone you can trust. When asked how these relationships are similar to family, she had this to say:

> My family, if you tell somebody one thing then they'll tell the other person and then everybody in the family knows your business. Same with my friends – well, some of my friends. With my mentor, it's just like whatever we say in between each other, it stays in between us.

Marshauna is comfortable sharing her feelings with her mentor but, because the mentor has not explained her own experiences, is unsure if she really relates to her circumstances. She believes the neighborhood surrounding the Community Youth Center is safe — the center's presence does a good job of helping prevent crime. She says:

> They teach you new lessons and get you more involved and stuff, to where you have things to do and you can't get in trouble if you have other things to do and not hanging out with those friends that get you in trouble.

Marshauna is also comfortable inviting her mentor to her home and visiting her mentor's home because they have developed a level of trust — only positive experiences with her mentor. She believes her mentor has the capacity to help her escape her circumstances by redirecting her path toward a more positive one. The people who have provided her the greatest inspiration are her grandmother, mother, and Michael Jordan. She said:

> I said my mom because she's been through a lot but she's pushing harder, she never gave up. My grandma because she's encouraged me and helps me do my best and not let me give up. Michael Jordan because even though he wasn't that good of a basketball player at first, he kept trying and he got better.

INTRODUCING SHAUNDREL-18

Shaundrel is a good kid with no juvenile justice system involvement. According to the Program Coordinator he is one of their longest-standing members but is in the Extend-a-Hand Program due to poor academic performance. She provided some insights into his academic struggles and family background stating:

> Shaundrel struggles a lot academically. So I know his background, he has an IEP, an individual learning plan, so academics is a huge thing for Shaundrel. Just a little background and I'll just touch on academics, family, and then general behavior or whatever. Yes, he struggles academically. He's actually behind so we're working with him one-on-one to make sure that he can graduate in May because he's a senior. He's 18. So his biggest thing now is graduating in May and finding a job. Just family background, Shaundrel comes from a large, very large family. He has very little involvement with his dad. I believe – I know that his dad has about 11 other children so his dad isn't really that involved with his life. And that's something that has been documented and we kind of had conversations with that about how he struggles with his relationship with his father.

According to the Program Coordinator, he struggles with authority and is hesitant to listen. One night the researcher observed him negatively responding. The staff member was trying to clear the gymnasium for the evening — he continued to play and expressed his discontent but eventually exited without further disruption. Despite some family dysfunction, his mother is extremely supportive. The coordinator said this about her support:

> His mom calls all the time making sure that he's in the homework room, that if he's here he's looking for a job. If he messed up or had an incident at school, she makes sure that he's not playing – he's not here playing basketball that he's here to get his work done. So his mom has been a huge support system just with him in the program and making sure that he's on track.

THE INTERVIEW

Shaundrel stated he is growing up in a single-parent home with two younger sisters. He lives in a violent community inundated with gang activity. He believes mentoring offers someone to look up to and willing to help whether academically or with other issues. Over the years he has had several mentors and has one now, but when he was first introduced to mentoring he was unsure what to expect, so he was scared and shy. Now he is more comfortable with the mentor-mentee relationship. He has attended the Community Youth Center for seven years and believes it helps keep him off the streets and work toward future life goals. He is an active member of Extend-a-Hand, Men-of-Change and the basketball team. He believes a good mentor helps his mentees academically and supports them in the development of life goals. He believes a bad mentor is someone who does not communicate or help his mentees academically. When asked his mentor choice as it relates to race, ethnicity and gender, he initially stated he had no preference but when asked if he would be comfortable discussing sex with a female mentor he said, "It depends." He enjoys the Extend-a-Hand Program and other programs offered at the center. When asked how he felt when he heard the term "at-risk" he stated:

> Like I'm being watched — Like, "Hey, you at-risk," and then you feel like I'm being watched, like I'm isolated.

His short-term goals are to graduate and get an apartment and in the future to earn an Associate's degree. Shaundrel values the mentoring program and feels fortunate the center is willing to offer this support to the community. He believes mentor and family relationships are similar — you can disclose personal things in hopes they can offer some guidance. However, he has some reluctance with sharing his personal thoughts with his mentor because he does not have confidence he can trust him completely. He believes his mentor can relate to his circumstances but he has to make sure he tells him exactly what it encompasses. He believes the community surrounding the center is extremely dangerous due to gun violence, gangs and its location. He believes the center does help reduce violence stating:

> Because I can see it for myself or Terrell or somebody, and say it like, "What if we weren't here?" Like if we weren't in the center, then we could be out somewhere playing with a gun or fighting or something like that.

He is uncomfortable visiting his mentor's home or to allow him to visit his home because he feels they have yet to establish a relationship that would warrant such an interaction. The most positive, enjoyable experiences he has had with his mentor was when they went fishing and hunting. He expressed no disappointments in his current or past mentor-mentee relationships. He believes his mentor has the capacity to help him escape his circumstances by teaching him the necessary skills needed to overcome them like focusing on his academics. When asked who has inspired him the most, Shaundrel replied:

> Probably my mom. Because she gave me my life, and I know she wants me to do good, like do better than what she did. So, I use that as motivation.

Introducing Marcus-17

The Program Coordinator and other staff members seem to have a strong desire to see Marcus excel, so he was one of the first participants the researcher got to know. During the observation period his attendance was sporadic at best, but once the basketball team was formed his attendance no longer fluctuated. He has no IEP and does not struggle academically. He is supposedly Terrell's cousin, but staff members are unsure if the familial connection is accurate. He is fairly new to the center. The Program Coordinator offered an overall assessment of his background stating:

> Marcus has probably one of the best family structures in the program, which is surprising because a lot of people that have come from two-parent households, they don't have behavior issues like he has. Marcus has a two-parent household. I think his dad actually owns a cellular phone company so they're very well off. He just chooses to, you know, like ignore all that. I don't even think – I'd have to check his address, but he's not even from this area. But Marcus is from a two-parent house-

hold. He is very well off. I've met his mom several times; she's a very nice lady, very supportive of him. She loves her son. Similar to Marion, he has support but when he's with his peers he chooses to be tough and have this life that he has. And when he was referred here is because he had got into an accident, like with a stolen car, and then a couple weeks before that he had just got expelled for fighting with a knife. He had a knife on him. After they broke up the fight they found a knife and he got expelled because he was on school property. He said, "Me getting kicked out of school, and me being caught with a stolen car," he said, "I ain't never did anything, nothing like that and it was an eye-opener for me." So he knows better.

Marcus has a temper. During the observation period his temper was on full display, evidenced by him pushing a chair and punching a wall. He had to be redirected by staff and share why he was upset. Marcus, who has had infractions with the law, has had none since joining the program; however, he was suspended twice for fighting. The Program Coordinator believes it is easier to advocate when the student is at the center but when their behavior is disruptive at school, the center is less likely to have a positive impact. The Program Coordinator hopes he learns to manage his anger, finish high school and perhaps go on to college.

THE INTERVIEW

Marcus grew up near the Community Youth Center in a two-parent household. His dad is from Ohio but lives in Memphis. He does not currently live near the center and thinks his community is relatively good and void of violence and gangs. He believes mentoring is the ability to get help from people at work. Prior to his involvement in the Extend-a-Hand Program, he never had a mentor. So his first mentor experience began at 17 and he did not feel any particular way about being assigned a mentor. He was a member of the center years ago but was kicked out twice — but does not remember what prompted his dismissals. He states he now comes to the center to do homework and play basketball (he is on the team). In addition to playing basketball, he is a part of Sports Alliance which helps him to develop his physical agility and strength. He thinks a good mentor-mentee relationship is one in which the mentor tries to help the mentee. Conversely, when a mentor offers little or no help and support, he believes is an example of a bad mentor. He does not have a preference about the race, ethnicity or gender of his mentor and would have no issue discussing sex or personal matters with a female mentor. He likes the Extend-a-Hand Program because he thinks it is fun and offers lots of activities like skating on Tuesdays. When asked what the term "at-risk" means he stated he did not know its definition. The researcher explained the definition as someone who has high risk factors like low-income, substance abuse, single-parent homes and communities with high drop rates. Once he understood the term and its implications he stated, "Uncomfortable. Because you don't know, like, you gotta watch out — watch what you do. Like you being targeted." His short-term goal are to finish school and to one day become a construction worker. He did not fully answer the question about whether he valued mentor relationships, but later disclosed that he sees his mentor infrequently due to his lack of cooperation and the mentor's inconsistency.

It is important to note he disclosed his recent mentor-mentee relationship was relatively new being a little over a month old. He believes mentor-mentee relationships are different from family because you grew up with them and have more comfort talking about personal issues. Hence, he finds it difficult to talk with a mentor about his innermost thoughts. He believes his mentor cannot relate to his upbringing because he did not come from the same background nor did he have the similar experiences. He believes the community around the center is somewhat safe, but because he grew up in the neighborhood he knows what happens in the community. When the researcher asked that he further explain the activity in the community he said, "Like, I don't even — I don't want to talk about that." Despite his lack of disclosure he did state the center helps to reduce crime, violence and dangerous activity in the community stating:

> Because, instead of being – as soon as you get out of school, being outside on the streets, you can come here. And do better. Do, like, programs and activities and stuff like that.

He would be comfortable visiting his mentor's home and he would invite his mentor to his home. Seeing that his mentor-mentee relationship is not yet developed he had no positive or disappointing experiences. Although he believes a mentor has the capacity to help him escape the realities of his circumstances, he is being intentionally resistant to forming a mentor-mentee relationship. We concluded the interview by expressing that his older cousin is his greatest inspiration because he keeps him out of trouble.

Introducing Terrell-15

Terrell is a dynamic kid whose charisma is enigmatic — not only do members flock to him, but the staff seems pretty fond of him, as well. The Program Coordinator had this to say about Terrell:

I usually don't have favorites, but Terrell is literally mine. If I had to pick a kid that I love more every day it would be Terrell. It's just his behavior. Terrell is a very good kid. I always call him a big baby. But his family and how he was raised shape so much of who he is, just his stepdad and his mother, they shape so much his character, that I don't really think that he feels like he can be himself.

His behavior has drastically improved but he was referred to the Extend-a-Hand Program because of his involvement with law enforcement. About a year ago he was involved in a mob action fight. According to the Program Coordinator, he is not afraid of violence. The coordinator offered a telling story about his stepfather saying:

> He even tells me like his stepdad blessed him into the gang, he blessed his friends into the gang. They kind of advocate for that – I've tried to meet with his mom before to sign some paperwork. She was already high in the car smoking weed trying to sign the paperwork. I think that if his family background and structure was better, he would have a better attitude, but his family structure is so dysfunctional he never had a chance to be Terrell because he had to be whatever his stepdad, his mom or his dad wanted him to be. And his dad, actual dad is in jail. He gets out this summer and he does not have a good relationship with him at all. I've already tried to talk to him. He's just like, "My daddy never did nothing for me." He got suspended one time for fighting in school and I said, "Well what'd your mom do about you being suspended?" He said, "She called my daddy while he was in jail." And I said, "So what your daddy say?" He said, "He tried to discipline me. He ain't had nothing

but the sixth grade education. He can't tell me nothing about high school." He has so much resentment to the point where his father can't do anything for him because he's just like, "you weren't there" kind of thing.

In addition to his family dysfunction, Terrell has a son named Quinton. The Program Coordinator asked him who he loves in his family and he responded, "I love my son." The Program Coordinator is under the impression he is in conflict with his child's mother so Terrell doesn't talk about Quinton often — this seems a frustrating, disappointing issue. Although one day he entered the center and found the Program Coordinator and said:

> "Man, look at these shoes." I remember him telling me he was so happy and I'm going, "Where did you get those shoes? What's in that box?" He's like, "I got these shoes for my son, you've gotta see them." They were Jordan's. I'm like, "Where you get all that money from to get your son some shoes?" He's like, "Don't worry about it, don't worry about it. Just know he good, he good." And it was just so cute because he just found something to love on, you know, and I was happy for him because in his mind, he buying his son a pair of shoes is just the best fathering thing ever he could do in his life.

The neglect and dysfunction he endures on a daily basis seems overwhelming from the Program Coordinator's perspective. She was reminded of another time when he was expressing his mother's lack of parental involvement saying:

> He told me one time, he's like, "Man, I've been up since 1:00." No, he's like; "I was up all night, 1:00." I said, "What you doing

up?" I'm like, "Your momma let you stay up that late?" He's like, "She don't care."

The lack of involvement from Terrell's parents makes it difficult for him to listen to authority figures especially when his parents condone and even encourage his poor choices. In addition to his family dysfunction he has ADHD (Attention-Deficit/Hyperactivity Disorder), so he has an IEP largely due to his struggles with it. He attends an alternative school and has shown some improvement there.

The Interview

Terrell was raised in a single-parent home with his older brother. When asked about the neighborhood where he was raised, he stated:

> I was raised in a bad gang related neighborhood. Lot of shootings and – shootings going on throughout the community, throughout the years of me growing up, and – yeah.

He believes his current community is still violent, but not as much as it was a couple years ago, and is not as bad as how he was raised. He believes a mentor is someone who is older and helps with homework and other things designed to assist the mentee in improving their behavior or academics. His previous experiences with mentoring programs have helped him in school. When asked about his first mentoring experience he stated:

> My first time I was introduced to mentoring? It was through Big Brothers Big Sister program. They used to always come to house, or we used to go to the library, help me out with my homework, and we used to go to fun places, or whatever I liked to do.

Terrell has attended the center for two years and simply comes to stay out of trouble. He is involved in Extend-a-Hand, Men of Change and the basketball team. He believes a good mentor is someone who checks on you weekly and provides any needed assistance. Conversely, he believes a bad mentor is someone who does not check up on you or assist you with homework. He doesn't have a preference of the race, ethnicity or gender of his mentor and would feel comfortable discussing topics like sex with a female mentor. He enjoys Extend-a-Hand and believes it helps him to stay off the streets and out of trouble and has helped him to improve his grades. Initially when asked what the term "at-risk" means, he was unaware of its definition. The researcher explained the definition as someone who has high risk factors like low-income, substance abuse, single-parent homes and communities with high dropout rates. Once he understood the term and its implications he stated, "Paranoid and stressed." His short-term goal is to keep his grades up and be promoted to the next grade. His long-term goals are to stay out of trouble and graduate from high school. He strongly values mentoring relationships stating:

> Oh. Yeah, they're important because a lot of kids need help and they just need someone to be there to talk to about their problems and just want to be there to help them with their work or whatever.

He believes mentor relationships are different than family relationships because mentors are not always around whereas family is permanent. He also believes it is easier to talk with family about everything and sometimes with your mentor he does not feel as comfortable. Hence, he struggles with sharing some of his innermost thoughts with his mentor because the duration and quality of the relationship is not strong. He believes his mentor semi-relates to his upbringing because he too grew up in a single-parent home. He believes the neighborhood around the center is not safe, but he does believe the center helps reduce crime and violence by keeping kids off the streets. He is not comfortable inviting his mentor to his home or visiting his mentor's home and would prefer to meet him in the library or somewhere else other than their respective homes. His most positive experience with his mentor was when he helped him finish a project for school. His most disappointing experience is when his mentor fails to check on him weekly. He does, however, believe his mentor has the capacity to help him escape the realities of his circumstances stating:

> By helping me do what I need to do to graduate high school and go to college and graduate college, and probably starting my own business, or help me in a way I can get money to, I mean like to help my neighborhood or my community.

His brother is his greatest inspiration saying:

> He's in college. He, he has two jobs. He, he moved out of town. Like four or five years ago. Yeah, he goes to the – he lives in Austin. He goes to like University of Texas. Oh wait, he's going for arts and graphic design.

INTRODUCING CORTEZ-16

According to the Program Coordinator, Cortez does well academically, has no IEP and has had no infractions with law enforcement. He used to attend the Community Youth Center years ago and has only recently returned due to his displays of anger at school. His mother is extremely supportive and works with the center to ensure that her son is behaving. His father is absent from his life and has 11 other children

— ironically all the boys are named Cortez. The coordinator interjected that she had met one of Cortez' mentors, who concurred that his temper was explosive:

> I've also met with a mentor of Cortez. It was a guy from the school district who said he's been mentoring Cortez since he was younger and he literally has had the same observations that I have had. Cortez is a good kid when he's good, but when he's bad it's bad. His temper-if I had to put a scale out of the 40-50 plus students that I work with, he would probably be like No. 2 on the list. That's how 0 to 100 his temper is. I actually had him in this one corner one time because it was just too much, like he was just screaming at the top of his lungs, chairs flying. It was ridiculous. 0 to 100.

On one particular occasion the researcher also observed his temper. It was simply astonishing — he was pacing back and forth with his fists tightly clinched. He had to be barricaded off by staff to halt his movement. It took about twenty minutes for the staff to calm him and control the incident. He eventually took a seat in the multipurpose area and remained under the supervisor of staff until his mother arrived. The researcher, curious to know what triggered his anger, believes it was either a reaction to not getting his way or being falsely accused.

THE INTERVIEW

Cortez contends he was raised well and had no struggles. He lives with his mother and stated he spends time with his father everyday but he seemed to alter his response saying, "Or every time I need him." He says he lives in a quiet neighborhood. He believes mentoring is when someone looks out for you. He believes he has a good mentor because he helps him with his grades and keeps him out of trouble saying:

> Like sometimes – like I usually get in trouble a lot at school, this has been my mentor I started third grade, and he helped me with my behavior problems, so it's like tenth grade now I don't get in trouble like that anymore. I know how to stay to myself and keep it, keeping my own, what I have up here, in my mouth, and I stop speaking my mind.

Cortez indicates he has had a mentor since third grade but initially he didn't care about having a mentor even though he came to talk to him two times per week. Now that he is older and his mentor owns a business, he talks to him once a week but Cortez wishes it was more frequently. He just returned to the center at the beginning of the school year and believes it helps keep him off the streets saying, "ain't nothing out there for you."

He is involved in Sports Alliance and Extend-a-Hand. He believes a good mentor helps out with many things like school and behavior. He thinks a bad mentor is someone who doesn't help and does not talk to the mentee. He does not have a preference of race, ethnicity or gender and would feel comfortable talking to a female mentor about sensitive topics like sex. When asked if he liked the Extend-a-Hand Program, he stated he was unsure why he is in the program and what it entails. When asked what he feels when he hears the term "at-risk" he said, "It's like you're taking that chance, you're risking yourself, you taking the chance." His short-term goal is to graduate next year. His long-term goals are to attend college, play basketball and be successful. His ultimate goal is to be an engineer or play in the NBA. He values mentor-mentee relationships and believes it is important to be respectful. He has a close bond to his mentor and believes the relationship is similar to a parent-child because his mentor is always looking out for his best interests. He shares a lot with his mentor and has no problem sharing some of his innermost thoughts. They have had personal conversations about his mother like when she was hospitalized. He believes his mentor has the capacity to help him escape his circumstances saying:

> He helped me a lot. He can tell me that I can get through it. He really religious person. He tell me like Jesus won't put me through nothing that I couldn't handle, and stuff like that.

He believes the neighborhood around the center is safe but when you go a little further into the community it is violent — he described it as, "hectic-a lot of shootings." He believes the center reduces crime and violence but because there are so many shootings they probably can't make it all stop. He feels comfortable visiting his mentor's home and inviting him to his home, but had never really thought about it. He provided an example of the most positive experience he's had with his mentor stating:

> Most positive experience was when he took us to the Muhammad Ali Museum, me and his other mentees to the museum, and we had a lot of fun together.

The most disappointing experience was so many of his friends stopped coming around for trips and mentoring activities but he eventually got over it. He believes his mentor has the capacity to help him escape his reality and offers an example of his assistance stating:

> He tell me every day he come get me. He ask me, like do I have any missing work and to go get my work, we, like we usually

go to lunch, he take me to lunch and then we come back to school and eat, but like some days we don't eat because I got to get some work together and we do it in the mentor office.

His greatest inspiration is his teacher, Ms. Riley, because she helped him pass his classes last year.

Introducing Jason-15

Jason is fairly new to the Community Youth Center and was referred to participate in the Extend-a-Hand Program by the Youth Assessment Agency. He does well academically and has no IEP, but he struggles to stay focused around his peers. He comes from a stable two-parent home. The Program Coordinator had this to say about him family:

> His home very good. His mom, very supportive, at every basketball game. Dad is there every basketball game. We had an orientation, mom and dad was there, sisters were there. You know, so his family background is very close-knit.

The primary reason he is at the center is that he has a juvenile case for retail theft. Prior to his arrival at the center, his peer circle was destructive causing him to make poor decisions, but he has since changed his group of friends and has not gotten in any more trouble. The Program Coordinator talked with his mother recently and stated:

> I just recently talked to his mom maybe a week ago and she's just like, since he's been at the center he's been doing phenomenal, as far as like behavior wise. She hasn't had any behavior issues with him or whatever and I think it's because he's just in a better place. He has better people to hang around with, he

doesn't feel the need to, like, do things to get in trouble. You know, because he's at the center every day.

Overall Justin is doing great, but as a consequence of his prior behavior, he is required by the court to comply with certain requirements to avoid being charged for retail theft. He is a typical teen — somewhat goofy and uncoordinated. Prior to the interview he proudly walked over to the researcher with a huge smile and said, "My friend told me I should talk with you, sir, so can I do the interview?" He hasn't shown any level of disrespect to staff members or his peers, but still finds himself playing too much and has to be redirected.

The Interview

Jason explained he was reared in a two-parent home until his parents separated but he has had a stepfather who has been there since birth — so his home always had two parents. He is originally from Missouri and only recently moved to Prairie Urban. He has no idea where his biological father is. He states his current community is good and does not have any crime or shootings. He believes mentoring is when someone gives advice and you can learn from it. When asked about his previous experience with mentoring and how he was first introduced to the mentor-mentee relationship he stated:

> I've been having a mentor ever since 5th grade. He comes every day to my school and talks to me and stuff like that. It's been for a long time. We just talk about my grades and behavior and all that I wasn't really introduced. I was just seeing a lot of people with a mentor, and back then, I was like, "Oh, this is gonna be fun. We'll probably just play. I get out of class and stuff." But then once I just started getting into it, I actually just learned

what it really is, and then I just started liking having a mentor.

He has been coming to the center on-and-off since he was in the 6th grade but stopped coming because he was involved in other activities. The primary reasons he comes to the center are to be on the basketball team and to do his homework. He proudly reported, "My grades are fully up because I've been doing work here." He is involved in the Extend-a-Hand Program and is on the basketball team. He believes a good mentor is someone who gives advice like staying out of trouble and doing well in school. He believes a bad mentor is someone who is not involved with the mentee — does not come to hang out and does not really try to help. When asked if he had a preference for a mentor he stated:

> Nope, it doesn't really matter to me because I literally can look up to anybody if I can relate to them and if I can know what they're saying and stuff.

He went on to say he would not have any issues talking about sex or other sensitive issues with a female mentor. Although he just started the Extend-a-Hand Program, he thinks it is pretty fun especially because they do a lot of activities. When asked about how he feels when he hears the term "at-risk" he stated:

> At-risk like danger or something, like something bad is about to happen, or it's already happened, or something like that. It makes me aware. If someone says, "You're at-risk," or something, I would be aware and know. I would feel bad because that means I'm not being a good role model or something.

His short-term goal is to receive A's and B's — maintain a 3.5 GPA. His long-term goals are to graduate from high school, attend college and play basketball or football in college. He values mentor relationships because he learns new things including right from wrong. He believes mentor relationships and family are similar stating:

> With certain mentors, it's like the same because I could talk to them or tell them how I feel or something, and I'll be good. It's basically like I talk to my parents. If I can't talk to my parents, I could talk to the mentor.

He is comfortable sharing his innermost thoughts with his mentor given they are close and have established a trusting relationship. He believes in order for his mentor to relate to his circumstances or situation, he has had to have gone through a similar situation or at least know someone who has, and if he does not, it would be unlikely he could relate. He believes the neighborhood around the center is safe and the center helps reduce crime and violence because it keeps kids out of trouble. He is comfortable visiting his mentor's home and inviting him to his. His most positive experiences with his mentor have been going to various places like banquets and other fun activities. He has not had any disappointments with his mentor-mentee relationship and believes his mentor is capable of helping him escape his circumstances. His greatest inspiration is his older brother.

INTRODUCING DESTINY-14

Destiny has been coming to the Community Youth Center on-and-off for a while. She was referred because she was going through an adoption and was placed with her aunt. She does well academically and doesn't have an IEP. According to the Program Coordinator she is one of the smartest kids at the center. Her biggest struggle is being a part of an extremely dysfunctional family. The Program Coordinator had this to say about her family:

> Her family is very dysfunctional and that's kind of why she's here for that support. So I know recently probably about four or five months ago she was adopted – she was taken from her mom and her dad just because of drugs and alcohol. It was terrible. They didn't have anywhere to sleep, they were sleeping on the floor. And this is what was told to us when she came to the center, under no circumstances are her mom or dad allowed to pick her up, they cannot. We have her court documents in her case management file because we need to keep that on file just in case her dad tries to pick her up. The same day that they signed the papers for her to be taken away, she was just like "I'm running away, I don't wanna live with my aunt," because they took her to her aunt. And she was like, "I don't wanna be at the center, I'm not staying here. They can't tell me who I can live with, they can't tell me that." And so when she first got here she struggled a lot because she was still adjusting to living with different family members.

When Destiny first returned to the center, she often talked about running away but over time she has developed a better attitude. Her relationship with her aunt has improved slightly, but according to the Program Coordinator her aunt uses drugs. Destiny has also reported that her aunt has stolen money from her on several occasions, including a $50 gift card she won in a raffle. Destiny believes she was placed in the home simply because her aunt had a house, not because the environment was less toxic. She has no juvenile justice involvement. Her aunt picks her up every day from the center.

THE INTERVIEW

When asked how she was raised she sternly said, "Nicely, rudely," She grew up in a single-parent home with her mother but now lives with her aunt but excitedly reports that it's only temporary. She says her relationship with her mother is good but with her dad, terrible. When asked how her relationship with her dad makes her feel she said, "Terrible!" When asked about her community she said it is irritating and she doesn't like it. Her understanding of mentoring was basic — she stated it was when someone mentors you but did not provide any specifics even when prompted. She states she has never had a mentor despite being involved in the Extend-a-Hand Program which has a mentoring component. When asked about other mentor programs like BBBS, she stated her uncle is trying to sign her up for that program. She has never had a mentor to her knowledge. She has attended the center since she was in the 6th grade. She comes to the center to get away from her aunt because she is irritating. She is a part of the Extend-a-Hand Program which she thinks is okay and Sports Alliance which she does not like. She believes a good mentor will help her with her homework and make sure she gets home safely. She had this to say about her perception of a bad mentor:

> Cursing me out, yelling at me, trying to slap me, being rude and not doing anything, just being on her phone or his phone.

When asked what type mentor she wanted, she stated she would prefer the same race and gender. She says her mother and auntie do not want her around men because they might try to do something to her. When asked how she feels about the term "at-risk" she said, "Sad and mad." Her short-term goal is to receive good grades in school. Her long-term goal is to graduate from college. Although she has not had any mentor relationships, she believes they are okay. However, when explaining the difference or similarity of a family member and a mentor she had this to say:

> They're (mentors) pretty nice in a visit. They visit you like three times – twice a week and family members, some of them don't even like you. Some of them don't even wanna be around you. Some of them are just rude.

When someone displays rudeness toward Destiny it makes her angry and she often responds impolitely. She would be comfortable sharing her innermost thoughts with her mentor once they have formed a trusting relationship. She believes her mentor can only relate to her upbringing if she tells them about everything she has experienced but she is concerned if that the mentor could not relate unless their experiences were similar. She believes the neighborhood around the center is okay — sometimes it's good and sometimes it's bad. She believes the center cannot reduce crime and violence, although they try. She would not feel comfortable inviting her mentor to her home saying:

> I would never bring my mentor around my auntie. If it's my mom, it's different. If it's my auntie, no. I'm never bringing anybody to my auntie's house. She talks too much. She's just irritating. She just talks too much. You don't even want to be around her. She won't even let you leave the house. If the mentor's in a good predicament with their family member then I'll go to their house if it's up to my mother.

Since she has not had a mentor she has not had a positive or disappointing experience. She believes her mentor would have the capacity to help her escape her circumstances. When asked who she felt was her greatest inspiration she surprisingly said, "Technically, my auntie even though she's irritating she's still helped me a lot and my mama." The researcher was shocked by her response and asked why she continually said her auntie was irritating and was it because she talked too much. Destiny said:

> It's not the talk she says it's how she acts and how she be around people. She tries to call me a dike and all of that. She calls me a bull dike. I said, "I thought you was just gonna say it around certain people. You weren't just gonna say it around people that I don't even know." She goes out and tells my business to other family members that go tell my business to other people. She claims that I don't have business, but I do have business because it's my business. They don't need to know all of that. Only certain people – technically my mom and my dad, the rest of them don't have to know.

Introducing the Staff (Program Director, Coordinator and Associate)

The Program Director has been with the Community Youth Center for nearly five years. His demeanor is enigmatic. The researcher observed him many times leaning into the table engaged in a rich dialogue with various teens. He is quick to share his wisdom and advice with youth. His approach is always without harsh rebuke and encourages the youth to utilize self-reflection to analyze their behavior. He moves with purpose and is clearly under a great deal of pressure but he never shuns the youth. He always makes them feel like they matter.

Eugene L. Moore, Ph.D.

The Interview-Program Director

The Program Director has a master's degree. He oversees operations for the Community Youth Center and performs other duties as required. He provides the following reasons why he joined the center:

I agree with the mission. Our mission is to enable all youth, especially those who need us most, to reach their full potential as responsible, productive, and caring citizens. My previous experiences are from running community centers for the Park District, Juvenile Detention, and other youth at-risk programs. The Community Youth Center provided me an opportunity to take the most holistic approach in serving the youth in our community, or any community, and I really believe in that; that embodies everything that we do. To enable them; to provide opportunities for them to learn and develop; for them to have an opportunity to work with caring adults. A lot of youth in every community struggle during the after-school times, and times when school is not in session, with having places to go or finding things to do. Just providing those opportunities and enlightening them. One of my favorite sayings is that you can't aspire to be anything you've never seen. So providing that opportunity through the caring adults or recreational opportunities or programmatic obviously is going to teach us what's important to help a child reach their full potential.

He believes mentoring is a helpful tool — it provides leadership and guidance and can happen in many forms. And he believes we all have mentors in some capacity. He believes the role of the mentor is providing food for thought and not making decisions for those being mentored. When asked to define "at-risk", he seemed to ponder how he would approach answering the question, and said:

> At-risk? Well, the Community Youth Center and most programs are based upon risk factors; family background, demographics, etc. For me, it could be a variety of things. Just because you're from an affluent area doesn't mean that you're not at-risk. It could be that you're lacking in whatever department can classify you as being at-risk.

The researcher was struck by his response and asked had he ever been labeled "at-risk". He responded, "Yeah" but added that at the time he was unaware that he was at-risk. He also mentioned that his job presents a lot of challenges, but clearly the most persistent one stems directly from the organization's nonprofit status — by definition funding and resources are built-in issues. He stated:

> Challenges is that it's a nonprofit, so funding and resources has always been an issue. Because the need is so great, and the ability to serve and have a holistic experience is a great challenge. The biggest reward is that I like to say "we do the impossible." We make the most for our buck from a business model. I take one dollar, and we get a dollar and twenty out of every dollar, and that's the goal. So that's the biggest reward is to take these challenges and make them into rewarding situations, like seeing a kid graduate from high school on time with a plan for the future, because that's our goal for every member. That's the biggest reward.

He recognizes that youth face many risk factors ranging from low-income to being brought up in a single-parent home. But being able to encourage kids to graduate from high school with a plan to become whatever they choose, gives him hope because he realizes that so many children are void of hope for their futures. Graduating from high school is only the first-step. He desires for youth to be excited to attend college, learn a trade or enter the workforce; and his mission is to serve as a caring adult who helps make those goals materialize. In his effort to provide youth with meaningful options for the future, he also believes parental and community support is invaluable saying:

> Parents play a huge role. One of the challenges, and I always like to use authority, is that sometimes it's challenging for us because we're telling our youth that they can become anything they want to. Some of the challenges with that is that to some individuals, that's not what they want their child to do. They want their child to do exactly what they do, whether it's the family business or whatever it may be. I like to look at it as parents getting involved with their kids at the center or any other type of community engagement, as beneficial because our community becomes better. If there's a young person that's in your family and they're struggling, they may consider attending the center because of your connection with me. The community gets a chance to see us working together and the youth know that we're all in this together. And the respect that you have may give me more respect, and the respect that I have may give you more respect. And you being in higher education and me working at the Community Youth Center is viewed differently; oh, the Program Director just works at the Community Youth Center. Well, you're obtaining a PhD. It's showing I know somebody that's obtaining a PhD that's successful, be-

cause that may be success for that kid. Or I know somebody who's a director at the center; that may be success for that kid. So parents having kids influenced by others makes the community better all the way around.

Initially the Extend-a-Hand Program only targeted youth 13-18 years of age, but he says the need to interact with youth much sooner is recognized — some kids are even being kicked out of elementary and middle school. He contends peer pressure is increasing bad behavior and without intervention youth will likely surrender to the negative pressure. The center tries to offer support from 7:30am – 9:00pm. The extended hours provide youth with assurance of the center's commitment and investment in their success. He contends that even when a youth sees a staff member after hours, perhaps crossing paths at the grocery store, the staff member is still making an impact. He provides details about mentor selection:

> We look for mentors all the way through. One of the challenges with the program is that we're in a transitional community. And what that means is that college students, when they come in and mentor, they're only there for three to four months, and then they graduate or go home for the summer. So one of the challenges we face is finding mentors who can stay at least for the whole year. Because once that relationship is established, the kid will have expectations and if you abruptly leave they will feel you abandoned them, which is one of their major concerns because everyone has left them or given up on them.

The center and director strive to eliminate a culture of abandonment. To help this goal the center solicits graduate students whenever possible to commit to the mentor-mentee relationship. Doctoral candidates are especially appealing because they are likely to provide longer-term service simply because of the time needed to finish their degrees. The Program Director provided some details on the training of mentors stating:

> We do provide training for them. We provide orientation, we provide fitness form, and we also provide an opportunity for input on how we can assist said youth. Part of the mentors' training is they meet with us for case management, because we do modified case management. That case management is to find out what's going on. So if Terrell is struggling, what is the real issue behind Terrell? It helps me as a director to deal with Terrell differently because I have more information on why Terrell is mad when he comes to the center. It could be because Terrell doesn't eat all day and he's coming angry because he's hungry. Me knowing that from a caring, trusted adult is better than saying hey, you're not following the rules, and getting kicked out of the place.

Programs are primarily developed from a national curriculum, but the Community Youth Center also develops programs based on community needs derived from strategic planning using a SWOT (strengths, weaknesses, opportunities and threats) analysis. To evaluate the effectiveness of programs, the center uses surveys, parent advising groups and enrollment numbers. Currently the center has a waiting list due to the overall demand for programs. We concluded our interview with the Program Director responding to his experience as a mentor and a mentee:

> I guess I would say the reason why I am a mentor is because of

what my mentors have done for me. When I was coming up and I'm just using the career; I'm not even going to go back to my adolescent years. Just in my career, politics is challenging if you don't have some guidance through it. It's like a mirror; things are bigger than they may appear. Things aren't what they appear in real life, in the real world. And having mentors to guide you through it and understand gives you perspective which was integral for me. You heard me use the word politics.

It's really not politics; it's really perception. We view things from our vantage point and that makes things what they are, but that may not be it because you have to understand everyone's role. Part of me being a mentor is helping kids understand a police officer's role, helping them understand what a teacher's role is. And understand it's not everyone's responsibility to do things for you; you have to help yourself. I always tell kids: "help me help you help yourself." That's the mode of mentoring and I want to know what's going on, and I want to help you help yourself to become everything that you would like to be. Because it's not about me; I'm here to help you. I want you to have the plan for the future. I want you to develop things you want to do.

And so that's kind of a philosophy, and that kind of details my experiences. I think a lot of mentors want their mentees to be like them, and mentoring really is not that for me. Mentoring is what that mentee wants. If that mentee wants to grow, we guide them and help them grow. And guess what, understanding we don't have all the answers, but we know some people who may have the answers for that particular youth along the way to help guide them. It's about putting everyone in the position to succeed. That's the philosophy, and that's what mentoring is to me.

THE INTERVIEW-PROGRAM COORDINATOR

The Program Coordinator chose to work for the Community Youth Center because it aligns with her interest in promoting positive youth development. Because she has a master's degree in social work and the center offers a variety of opportunities for youth, the position also allows her ample opportunities to advocate for the youths, exposing them to needed social services. The center gives her flexibility in programming and allows her the role of working with the population she prefers — the population the center currently serves. She stated her goal:

> The goal is to have all members on track to graduate high school or with a plan for the future. So just to work with kids individually and make sure they're on track, to encourage them to make sure they have some kind of plan for the future, and give them the tools to succeed, basically; just make sure they're being the best person that they can be.

The researcher asked what does a "plan for the future" look like and does that plan apply to those kids who do not finish high school and she responded stating:

> Yeah, either or. So of course I want them all to finish high school but some people just don't have either the resources or the interest, really, to finish high school. That path isn't always for everybody. So whether it's getting a GED and whatever

course you may have to be, whether it's going to an alternative school, or a trade school or whatever the case is so if they don't want or they can't make that direct path to just graduate high school, make sure that they have some sort of plan for the future and that it's a positive plan, and that it puts them on track for some kind of future ahead of them.

The Program Coordinator describes mentoring as working with individuals one-on-one or in groups, guiding them from her own experience and with other resources. Her goal is serving as a positive role model to help the mentee stay focused. Her biggest challenge is that the Community Youth Center is only a small part of the kids' realities — she in unable to always help the kids whose lives are filled with obstacles outside the center. Unfortunately, this challenge is compounded by parents who either are unwilling or incapable of encouraging their children to do their best. She finds joy when kids, despite the odds against them, show improvement. She cited this example with excitement:

Like just a couple days ago I had a kid that was struggling academically. I put him in alternative school because he was refusing to go to class, refusing to do any homework or anything. And his grades at his alternative school have been awesome; literally A's and B's. The entirely different setting was perfect for him. Now he looks forward to going to class. All of a sudden he said it's less strict so he feels more comfortable with engaging with the staff and the teachers there.

I was just happy to see his grades and to see his growth. Because at first, you think of a negative shift; "oh, my kids, they've got to go to alternative school"; they can't function in the public school. But in actuality, that may be a better space for some kids and I was just happy to see that that worked for him.

She said that the kids who attend the center seldom have just one risk factor. Members of the Extend-a-Hand Program come in on probation or are referred by the Youth Assessment Agency. One of their biggest areas of struggle is peer pressure, contributing to their poor behavior at school. In addition many come from dysfunctional families plagued with physical abuse, drug addiction or multifaceted problems. Many of the members of the Extend-a-Hand Program also live in single-parent homes. This risk factor warrants mentoring and works well with it because children from single-parent homes often are seeking positive role models. When asked how programs are developed and measured, she stated:

> We have a mandatory curriculum so we don't necessarily develop or create our own programs but we receive curriculum-based and evidence-based programs from our national office. Then we also document those programs and then we put them into a system. So the kids, they also do a pre-test and post-test before every quarter. The Extend-a-Hand program is a little different because we have case management as well so we can measure progress pretty quickly. For example, if I've been documenting in August that a kid has been struggling in biology, or has been struggling getting along with other kids. In September, October and November I am continuing to write case notes so in late November I would indicate if he's met a couple new friends, or he actually increased his F to a B.

She has experience as both mentor and mentee and often interacts with the kids playing basketball, taking them out to lunch and just trying to build positive relationships. She is not trying to be their friend, just serve as a caring adult. She believes the relationship is best formed by being transparent — offering insight into her upbringing and listening to them talk about their families. She has had multiple mentors throughout her life and values the relationships with every one of them. She explained the Extend-a-Hand Program and its structure:

> The Extend-a-Hand Program is a program through the Mental Health Association, so they funded us to do a program and work with an additional 40 kids. We received referrals for those kids, 13-18 year-olds from different community organizations that work with youth. However, some were already members of the center and enrolled in the program because they met the risk factors, not because of being referred due to juvenile justice. They would just come here to the center and we would provide them with programming, mentoring and case management to help them get back on track. A lot of times we work with the Youth Assessment Agency; that's probably one of our biggest organizations here that we work with. They have juvenile justice system adjustments, where if they come to the center a certain amount of times a week and they do their programs, they can drop the charges that they have. So we work with them. We also get kids directly from the police department and school district.

The only training mentors receive is an orientation, (this contradicts the director's remarks). The recruitment process is internal and it fairs at the local college and university, the park service, listserv, advertisements and word-of-mouth. Mentors are required to be at least 18 years of age, pass a criminal background check and agree to adhere to the rules, regulations and policies of the Community Youth Center. They seek mentors who are interested in youth development and are able to commit time at least once or twice a week. The mentor is assigned a caseload (that sees the same kids routinely) and typically performs the mentoring in a group setting. After the formal predetermined 12-question interview was completed, the researcher fielded one more question to the Program Coordinator: *How effective is the Community Youth Center in dealing with systemic issues like poverty, crime and violence?*

> I think that's a very interesting question because if we're talking about systemic issues, I think the center has very little chance of changing it especially poverty, crime and violence. That's very hard for the center to do. I think the center plays a huge role but a lot of times the parents don't wanna work with you. They don't want their family business out there, the kids feel like they don't have no issues. They don't even know what at-risk factor is. So when we have kids that are really interested in change and they wanna do better and they take advantage of the resources we have, we see a lot more progress as far as shifting and changing that. But a lot of times we don't get kids and families that are interested in that because a lot of them, they don't think they have an issue at all. They don't care, like "Cortez and them; they don't think that they got an attitude. He just pissed me off, that's why I'm mad. I don't have an attitude, you know what I mean?" So it's hard to work with them when they just don't wanna take advantage of the opportunity.
>
> Parental involvement is key, when you working with kids, because you can't do anything without them. There's so many things that you can't do without a parent unless you get, like I

said, those kids that are very self-motivated that have that confidence and that self-esteem. You don't get that from teenagers a lot. Very few kids that are able to control their own future themselves. You know, a lot of times they don't have that voice. Young people don't have that voice. They need parents, adults and mentors advocating for them and if we don't have that, we can't really do nothing about it. The center can't do anything if we don't have a parent or guardian or somebody advocating for that kid.

The Interview-Program Associate

The Program Associate actually began as a volunteer before being hired full-time. He finished high school and has taken some college courses. In his hometown of New Orleans, he worked with kids at his church, so when he came to Prairie Urban he was committed to making an impact in the lives of African-American children. When asked about what goals he had for the youth he serves he stated:

> So basically, I try to change their thoughts, their outlooks on everything negative that's going on in their life. So I have heart-to-heart conversations with each member and basically anything negative that's going on, I try to change that a little, change turning it positive. Show them steps that they could take, you know, to fix things like that.

He believes mentoring is providing one-on-one interaction with youth in which the mentor is sharing his knowledge about life to help the mentee make sounder, smarter decisions. When asked to define "at-risk" he stated:

> Wow. That's a good question. That's a good question. I mean,

society thinks "at-risk" is a kid that made a mistake, one mistake, and give him a title and they call that at-risk, an at-risk kid. Does he have an anger problem and at that second it went too far. I call things like that a mistake, but an at-risk kid is someone that's has no positivity. They don't want to change for nothing, you know. I feel like a kid that made one mistake is not at-risk. An at-risk kid is just reckless in their behavior and a kid who's made a mistake would be more of a proper term for the kid. I feel that society easily labels kids. They easily label kids, put a title on them if they're, you know. They put the title on them if they make one mistake, they say they're at-risk. Society labeled me at-risk but I labeled myself as determined.

His biggest challenge working in the center is dealing with a multitude of unresolved emotions, ranging from anger to hopelessness, that need to be acknowledged and addressed. He contends the greatest reward is when he has a breakthrough with a kid and sees him making a turn down the right path. He believes the biggest issue kids face is the need to fit in, which often results in the making poor choices. He did not answer any questions pertaining to the structure of the Extend-a-Hand Program because this is outside the scope of his duties. However, we concluded the interview with him talking about his childhood experience as a mentee:

My cousin, he's the pastor of my church back home. Amazing! So the experience was from about nine years old until I graduated from high school. He just explained to me that, you know, we are human. We make mistakes. You know, we can feel like we've been oppressed by the world. We can feel like nobody's in our corner. But the thing that he says the most is life goes on and you have to know, like you have to find that courage and that motivation. You've got to dig deep just to keep going with whatever situation or obstacle or shortcoming, you know, and just keep moving through that just to get to your goal.

These interviews provided a rich dialogue detailing the lived experiences of 10 at-risk teens participating in the Extend-a-Hand Program at the Community Youth Center. While their stories had eerie commonalities, there were also stark differences that add dimension to the mentoring debate. Their responses to the questions reflected the notion that no two stories are the same because individuals walking the same path each experience it differently. Even among the staff members, their views of mentorship varied and in turn influenced how they interacted with members of the Community Youth Center.

CHAPTER 5
DISCUSSION OF FINDINGS

The research study explores the mentor-mentee relationship through the lived experiences of at-risk teens participating in an after-school program in a micro-urban community. The term "lived experience" is used to describe first-hand accounts and impressions of living as a member of a minority or oppressed group. When the researcher started to account for all the things he was observing at the Community Youth Center, he wanted to ensure that the voices of the youth would not be lost in the chaos. The lives of twins Justin and Jalen, siblings Marion and Marshauna, Shaundrel, Marcus, Terrell, Cortez, Jason, and Destiny are far more dynamic than most could imagine. Their stories along with the feedback and insights of the staff helped answer the primary research questions that guided this study.

JUSTIN...

After reviewing the research notes and the interview transcripts of Justin and the Program Coordinator, it was clear that Justin faces some major hurdles — his immaturity and poor academics, and the high-risk factor, low-income. Using grounded theory, applied to the assessment from the Program Coordinator and to Justin's actual interview responses, five reoccurring themes were elicited —1) peer pressure, 2) low-income, 3) single-parent household, 4) family dysfunction and 5) negative connotations of being labeled "at-risk". These themes were evidenced in most of the teen participants. Problems arising from peer pressure mostly manifested while he was in school — despite his gentle and respectful manner, it did not prevent him from making poor decisions that ultimately resulted in disciplinary action. The Program Coordinator emphasized his low-income status stating that he and his brother were so extremely poor, that they were given support from donors to assist with clothing and other basic necessities. He also had to contend with the death of his mother when he was eleven. This undoubtedly affected him, but he was not forthcoming about this life-altering event. When asked about his mother, he showed reluctance to answer as if mourning or grieving her loss would inflict unwanted pain. The Program Coordinator contends that the Community Youth Center serves as a space of love, fun, and support for the twins. These factors are mostly missing in their home due to the age and the weakened mobility of their grandmother. Even Justin acknowledges one of his primary reasons for attending the center is to get out of the house and have fun. Family members like his uncle attempt to offer some support, but the majority of the weight and pressure to raise Justin and his brother sit on the shoulders of his elderly grandmother, whose commitment is unwavering despite her diminished capabilities.

Justin, like most of the participants of the Extend-a-Hand Program, is a product of a single-parent home. He seems to believe effective mentoring can overcome his presented challenges. Justin, like all the participants, took offense to the term "at-risk" expressing it makes him believe he did something wrong. The afore-mentioned five reoccurring themes were also present when interviewing Jalen with little variance, despite Jalen being deemed mature by the Program Coordinator, staff, and the researcher.

JALEN...

Jalen quickly endorsed mentoring. He believed his mother was intentional in getting him paired with an older non-familial adult to lessen the chances of him being engaged in poor activities in the streets. It was obvious he saw the Community Youth Center as a place of opportunity. His love for the center is evidenced by his strong involvement with programs. He really values mentoring likely due to his mother being so supportive of this intervention — now that she is gone it is even more important for him to have positive mentoring relationships. However, he has had frequent changes in mentors. The inconsistency, however, did not cause Jalen to believe these relationships have no impact. In fact, he contends such relationships are a wonderful idea. However, despite his raving of the mentor-mentee relationship, he expressed apprehension about sharing his innermost thoughts with his mentor. This admission led the researcher to believe that although he touted how positive and meaningful these relationships were, his comfortability with his mentor was insufficient — lacking in trust.

Jalen responds to peer pressure somewhat better than his brother but stills make an attempt to fit in with other members at the center. His ability to play basketball is less than, but he makes a valiant effort to contribute to the team by being aggressive on the court. His aggression is demonstrated by going after every loose ball and closely guarding his opponent. Since he and his brother are reared in the same home, he too grapples with the realities of low-income, single-parent household, dysfunctional family and being labeled "at-risk". He feels the term "at-risk" means imminent danger or harm. The Program Coordinator said Jalen performed better academically than his brother, but contends his accomplishments are actualized because of the center's support, not necessarily from his teachers or school. When expressing her sentiments about other participants, she concurred the center has less of an impact while the members are at school. This led the researcher to believe that uncontrollable factors in the schools — like classroom size, time and resources — prevent teachers from having the capacity to serve as mentors. Although schools offer in-school mentoring programs the environment seems less conducive to the members of the Extend-a-Hand Program. The Program Coordinator stated the participants enter the center very emotional due to their day at school and utilize the center to calm down. Jalen is no different as he enters the Community Youth Center — he is trying to escape the pressures of his school environment and the mundane reality his home life presents due to his ailing grandmother.

Marion...

Marion was extremely candid during his interview. Along with the information provided by the Program Coordinator, it quickly became evident his greatest challenge is his inability to withstand peer pressure. This was only a portion of his self-reported struggles. It was interesting to learn that despite his tendency to be easily influenced by his peers, he did not perceive himself as tough — which makes his getting into self-initiated fights somewhat peculiar. Like many kids just trying to fit in, he chose a group of friends that garner bad outcomes like school suspensions. He did not state any issues or concerns about his low-income status — this seems the norm for most teens at the center. The center accommodates the needs of low-income members nicely. For instance, many are provided basketball shoes if they do not have a pair that fit.

Another accommodation is waiving the nominal membership fee for those who cannot afford it.

Marion's single-parent household is stressful and oppressive. Despite his good relationship with his father, his childhood was set on the center stage of abuse. He watched helplessly as his mother was physically and emotionally abused by his father which lends credence to their family dysfunction. It is apparent this abuse caused Marion a significant amount of emotional trauma, despite having received help from a psychologist, and it appears to continue to haunt him. At school he succumbs to a great level of peer pressure; in contrast, he does not behave in a reckless or uncontrollable manner at the center. According to the Program Coordinator, his family's dysfunction is a huge obstacle for Marion — consequently, he treats his mother disrespectfully despite knowing it is unproductive and hurtful. Although others are aware of the tension between his mother and him, he does not acknowledge the emotional abuse he inflicts. Marion was not hesitant to express how he grew up in the face of horror — the abuse was so intense he felt like he could not protect his mother or sister. The tension between Marion and his mother was difficult to flesh out. At one point he candidly stated he wanted his mom to care for him, implying that he seeks her approval and validation. His interpretation of the term "at-risk" was associating it with someone in desperate need of help and recognizing the anxiety that would innately cause. Despite his being generally unaware of his risk factors, the continual abuse inflicted upon his mom when he was a child, caused great anxiety and emotional instability.

Marshauna...

Marshauna was reared to treat people with respect and dignity despite having been continuously bombarded with blatant disrespect from her father. She understands peer pressure is a major hazard for her because "when you hang with the wrong people" you are more likely to engage in inappropriate behavior. While she comes from a low-income family, she never mentioned this directly or any of the limitations this factor presents. Her brother and the Program Coordinator had both spoken of the dysfunction present in her family, but Marshauna mentioned only briefly that her parents were divorced. It was not apparent whether her omission of key facts surrounding her childhood was due to her uncomfortableness with the topic or because she is four years younger than her brother, thus probably having a less distinct memory of the abusive events. However, she did express her disapproval of family members who spread rumors or disclosed information that she had provided in confidence.

As for her thoughts about being labeled "at-risk", she stated, "I would feel offended." Those four words were not spoken in her normal, low and subdued pitch, but were voiced in anger. Her facial expression reflected her visceral disdain for the term as she rolled her eyes and tilted her head while responding to the question. This response was a clear deviation from how she had answered the previous questions. Her response prompted more awareness in the researcher as they described their understanding and reactions to the term.

Eugene L. Moore, Ph.D.

Shaundrel...

Shaundrel has attended the center for many years and struggles academically in school. The Program Coordinator indicated he is attempting to graduate from a traditional high school but is finding it difficult. She mentioned he has an IEP but did not indicate if it was due to a learning disability. He has the demeanor of a leader and when he is interacting with others, they seem to defer to his leadership. It was not clear how peer pressure affects him directly as he is somewhat reserved when talking about his personal life. He has a younger sister who attends the center and their relationship appears close as they go back and forth like typical siblings. Although Shaundrel has a slight temper, he is mostly well-behaved at the center. His behavior at school was not reported other than the IEP due to poor academic performance. His low-income status, while known, was not discussed in detail. He comes from a single-parent home with an extremely supportive mother encouraging him to graduate from high school. His family dysfunction is evidenced by his estranged relationship with his father who is believed to have 11 children. He expressed being labeled at-risk makes him feel like he is being watched and is isolated. Shaundrel is one of those kids everyone really wants to succeed but success is such a struggle. He contends the community is inundated with violent gang activity. He desires independence and wants to have an apartment while he pursues an associate's degree. He, like many of the teens, has a goal to attend college but with his struggles academically, college will likely present some difficulty if he does not receive some tutoring. He has goals like most teens — some typical, graduating from college and others more lofty, becoming a professional athlete in the NBA. However, having a well-articulated goal is not the same as having the resources necessary to help the goal materialize.

Marcus...

Marcus is well-liked by the staff at the Community Youth Center — the researcher also acknowledges his charisma and charm but it is enigmatic what exactly makes the attraction. The Program Coordinator indicated he does not struggle academically. He more often than not concedes to pressure from his peers and has a volatile temper that has gotten him into major trouble. He was expelled from school and has had numerous suspensions. As noted previously, the Program Coordinator's analysis of the teens occurred after the researcher interviewed the teens, so what was reflected in their case management reports was not always revealed during the interview. It is unclear why Marcus stole an automobile or fought with a knife but according to the Program Coordinator, it is largely due to peer pressure and his flaring temper. He is not considered low-income according to his case file, but the Program Coordinator emphatically stated he is not from the poor side of the tracks nor is he reared in a single-parent home. However, during the interview, he indicated that he was brought up in a single-parent home and his dad currently lives in Memphis, so it is likely he lives with his mother and stepdad, not his biological father. Despite living in a good neighborhood and having supportive parents, his family dysfunction is evidenced by the strained relationship he has with his biological father. The term "at-risk" makes him uncomfortable because he feels it forces him to be on guard like he is being watched. It is interesting to note Marcus was unwilling to discuss the criminal activity surrounding the center, but conceded that a diversion from school to the center would likely produce bad outcomes due to the violence present in the community. It is a mystery why he willingly engages in bad choices, yet he showed remorse for his previous infractions with the law. Maybe the

Program Coordinator has it correct to suggest his behavior is directly correlated to him having a negative peer circle and being pressured to engage in activities he knows are counter-productive. His negative peers are at school and when he comes to the center he does not engage in the non-productive activity.

TERRELL...

Terrell is a clear favorite of the Program Coordinator despite her calling him a bully on numerous occasions when he was dealing with his peers. However, she did contend he is not afraid of violence and is frequently the perpetrator. The Program Coordinator did not talk about Terrell's response to peer pressure, but she spent a great deal of time explaining the negative pressure displayed by his mother and stepdad. He stated he was brought up in a low-income neighborhood in a single-parent household. His greatest obstacle is the dysfunction his family presents. It was disheartening to learn his stepdad blessed him into a gang — an initiation of sorts. He definitely displayed restraint when answering questions. For instance, he did not disclose that he had a son, a contentious relationship with his biological father, or poor guidance rendered by his mother and stepdad. The Program Coordinator did indicate he has Attention-Deficit/Hyperactivity Disorder (ADHD). Perhaps his ADHD, coupled with his family dynamics and temper, explain some of the infractions he has at school. As mentioned in the interview, he attends an alternative high school where he has indeed shown some progress. The researcher believes Terrell wants validation from his stepdad and mother, as they often support him in his wrongdoing. His response to the term "at-risk" was interesting — it made him feel paranoid and stressed. It is evident the term "at-risk" causes concern for the teens and all were seemingly unaware they had been categorized as such. It was equally evident the teachers, scholars and the center staff all see them as at-risk and interact and respond to their needs based on that perception. Terrell, at 15 years of age, is living a life with adult responsibilities, but it is evident he too needs the same nurturing support he gives to his one-year-old son.

CORTEZ...

Cortez has had mentors for years. As stated earlier, he was referred to the Extend-a-Hand Program because of his severe anger displayed at school — the researcher also witnessed his intense anger on full display. However, when Cortez is not angry, he is a friendly, personable young man. When he was playing basketball and his team was not winning he would get very angry and begin to lose focus and interest in the game. The Program Coordinator attempted to bring some clarity as to why he demonstrated uncontrollable behavior, but it is still unclear what exactly causes Cortez's anger. Cortez acknowledged his behavioral problems and believes his mentor helping him develop the ability to calm himself down, has allowed him to minimize his school distractions. The Program Coordinator seems to struggle between Cortez being furious when he is misunderstood, accused or just wanting to have his way. Regardless of the cause, his behavior was unacceptable. When he displays anger at school, the behavior warrants an immediate suspension from school which seems to not have little capacity to calm Cortez down, unlike the center that will quickly rush to his aid. In the midst of his low-income, single-parent home, his estranged relationship with his father who has 11 other children adds to his family dysfunction. The term "at-risk" makes him feel like he is taking a chance with his life.

The researcher felt he explained it metaphorically like someone who is deemed at-risk lives his life walking a tightrope or jumping into a lion's cage during feeding time.

JASON...

Jason is a good kid. His primary issue is peer pressure, not home life. He comes from a stable, two-parent home where he lives with his mother and stepfather. While his family has stability, a potential concern is that he does not know where his biological father is. Nonetheless, it was interesting to compare his responses to those of the Program Coordinator who spoke highly of him. During his interview with the researcher, he was perhaps the most well-behaved and well-mannered participant. However, the researcher witnessed his behavior change when he was around his peers. Prior to conducting the interview, the researcher observed him talking with his peers, really trying to fit in by being active in the dialogue — this translated mostly into him simply being rambunctious. However, once he entered the interview he was calm and eager to answer the questions. At first, the researcher thought he was attempting to display a certain image because he was interviewing, but it became apparent that he alters his behavior when speaking with adult authority. He was eager to inform the researcher that he was doing well in school and aspired to get high marks. The Program Coordinator and his mother attest that his behavior has drastically changed since he has made a new group of friends. Prior, Jason was involved in a retail theft, largely because of the friends he was hanging out with. Seeing his need or acceptance, the wrong friends provided the perfect opportunity for him to do something that he clearly knew was wrong. Despite giving into peer pressure, the overall assessment from the researcher's perspective is that he is extremely impressionable. According to Jason, he can look up to anyone — this is perhaps why he was getting into unnecessary trouble. He, like most of the teen participants, took issue with the term "at-risk" and felt it made him feel like he was in danger. His explanation was perhaps the most detailed as he seemed to internalize the word and when the label was applied to him, he felt he was not being a good role model for others.

DESTINY...

Destiny is by far the most disheartening story the study features — she is contending with extreme family dysfunction. She lived in a single-parent home until she was removed by a court order due to her mother's drug abuse. The Program Coordinator shared a great amount of information pertaining to child protective services removing her from her home and placing her with her aunt, which Destiny vigorously opposed. In most cases, teen participants did not divulge personal stories that gave credence to their family's dysfunctions, but Destiny held back no punches when speaking of her family — in particular, her disdain for her aunt. Although many of her responses were short they were chilling. The relationship with her father, "terrible!" How she was reared, "Nicely, rudely!" How she describes her aunt, "irritating!" As the interview progressed she demonstrated some trauma — it seemed odd to the researcher that she felt a bad mentor would verbally assault and strike her, and be rude in their interactions with the mentee. Her one or two word answers, even when probed further, prompted the researcher to quit pushing more, concerned she may become emotionally agitated and perceive the follow-up questions as an interrogation rather than an interview. She stated that the term "at-risk" was saddening and upsetting. She also expressed that when someone treats her rudely she becomes angry.

The Program Coordinator provided insight into how the trauma of being removed from the home had made Destiny feel, but the coordinator would likely be shocked to learn of the verbal abuse Destiny has endured. It was incongruous and shocking to learn that she considered her aunt was an inspiration, despite revealing her aunt calls her a derogatory term used to describe her sexual orientation. She was less concerned about being called a "bull dike" but infuriated when her aunt would refer to her as such in the presence of others. Destiny never disclosed her sexual orientation, sexual abuse or any trauma she had experienced explicitly, but clearly, she is dealing with deep levels of abuse. Despite her mother's addiction to drugs, Destiny loves her and would prefer to be homeless with her mother than housed under the vitriolic scrutiny of her drug-free auntie.

Program Director...

It is obvious the members of the Community Youth Center are fond of the Program Director. He talks extensively about serving as a caring adult to vulnerable populations like the members who attend the center. He firmly believes providing kids with positive, productive options, is critical in supporting their advancement. His goal is to provide a plan for the future. The researcher, initially unsure what a plan for the future entailed, learned that it could range from going to college or learning a trade, based solely on the aspirations of each child. His definition of the term "at-risk" was relatively standard and included family background and demographics. But the most interesting aspect of his explanation was that he believed affluent kids could be labeled at-risk too. In addition to his definition, he stated that he was unaware as a child of his own high-risk factors — being brought up in a single-parent home and being born into poverty.

The challenges he faces at director level are likely similar to those of most nonprofit management — funding inevitably becomes the organization's Achilles heel. He expressed pride in his ability to stretch resources to serve more children. But the researcher contends that while the director's financial savviness is impressive, it is not sustainable. The most vulnerable kids receiving support from the center see the negative effects of limited resources — the negative effects of inadequate facilities and substandard conditions can lead kids to believe they are unworthy. Although he believes that the involvement of some parents is counterproductive and contradicts the values and aspirations the center is trying to instill in its members, he also believes that parental support is invaluable — it helps the center better engage with the community and provides a narrative that donors and sponsors would gladly support.

The researcher contends that good parental involvement would most certainly be a valuable asset, yet it is not the prevailing cause of program failure or for teens having no viable plan for the future. The Program Director believes peer pressure is forcing many kids down a path of destruction; and without some form of intervention, they will likely succumb to the effects of their poor choices. Finding quality mentors is a challenge — he aims to select mentors who can commit for at least one year to ensure members are not left with the effects of their premature departures. The researcher contends that the demographics surrounding the center also make retaining quality mentors more difficult. The Program Director provided some insight into the training mentors receive. The preparation did not appear extensive but did include an orientation and a fitness form. It is important that mentors are given the flexibility to offer suggestions that they believe would better serve their mentoring efforts. The most informative aspect of their training is the review of the case management notes, which provide the mentor-trainee needed context about the risk factors experienced by the prospective mentee(s). However, mentors need quality training to deal with the complex issues these kids face to ensure that they are not simply defining and seeing the mentees through the lens of their risk factors. For instance, the center can explain Destiny's anger is rooted in her experience of abuse, but in the end, how does the center's awareness truly help Destiny overcome her obstacles? Programs are based on a national curriculum.

The researcher contends these programs, while easily evaluated on a large scale, are not producing outcomes beyond some statistics and a few testimonials. Shaundrel coming to the center every day and getting involved in productive activities is indeed a successful outcome. The waiting list for children to join the center is a successful outcome or indication their programs have merit according to the Program Director but if Shaundrel does not complete high school or find meaningful employment how impactful were the center's efforts? The researcher agrees with the Program Director about the importance of mentors and community centers, but they slightly diverge on the notion of "mentoring being what the mentee wants," as it is evident the mentees have goals both immediate and long term, but what is not so clear is if they have the adequate resources to successfully see those goals come to fruition.

Program Coordinator...

The Program Coordinator's goals are similar to the Program Director — she desires all members to graduate from high school and have a plan for the future. She believes these goals are best achieved when members are provided opportunities designed to keep them on track. For those members who do not successfully graduate from high school, she will direct them (to other services) based on their goals and plans for the future. What happens to the member who cannot overcome his poor decisions — what does the future look like for that kid? It appears that mentoring serves as a positive intervention but according to the Program Coordinator, that positivity is often overshadowed by an unsupportive parent and the mounting obstacles the youth face. Simply put, the Community Youth Center cannot help all at-risk kids. She believes peer pressure is another major obstacle preventing at-risk youth from succeeding, coupled with having multiple risk factors. It is interesting both the Director and Coordinator find the greatest opportunity is the parents and the member's inability to withstand peer pressure, but do not account for the other prevailing factors which contribute to their misfortune, like systemic poverty, inadequate schools and oppression.

Despite these omissions which the researcher contends, they are aware exists, they seem to suggest 100% parental involvement and the ability to resist peer pressure would reroute the paths for kids deemed at-risk, but such an assumption is overly optimistic. Even when asked a more targeted question about how the center helps deal with systemic issues like poverty, she conceded that they had little chance to curtail its prevalence. In fact, she somewhat doubled down on the need to gather more parental support. She believes young people do not have a voice and need caring adults, parents, advocates, and mentors to provide support and guidance in conjunction with places like the Community Youth Center — without a collective effort, the center's impact is limited. But we need an even stronger effort from our elected officials to provide resources to eliminate poverty because clearly the Community Youth Center and similar organizations are not equipped to do so.

Eugene L. Moore, Ph.D.

Program Associate...

The Program Associate provided the strongest endorsement to eliminate the label "at-risk" as he feels it is debilitating. He believes the title alone places them on guard as others are watching their every move. The researcher agrees based on the teens' responses, the term is more than problematic — alternatively, some will argue it is no different than any other category designed to provide a deeper understanding of certain factors. However, we cannot ignore the voices of the very group the term targets to help — perhaps we need to look beyond risk factors and labels, and address instead the root cause, poverty that gives the term "at-risk" merit. The Program Associate also attests that members enter the center with many unresolved issues and their time at the center, while productive and fun, does little to solve them. Using grounded theory, the interviews produced five common themes —1) peer pressure, 2) low-income, 3) single-parent household, 4) dysfunctional family and 5) the offensive nature of the term "at-risk". These themes were discussed, analyzed and produced a greater understanding from the mentee's perspective, but did they effectively answer the primary research questions guiding the study?

The research study explored the mentor-mentee relationship through the lens of at-risk teens participating in an after-school program in a micro-urban community. When the researcher started to account for all the things he was observing at Community Youth Center, he wanted to ensure that the voices of the youth considered at-risk would not be lost in the chaos. At first, attempting to juxtapose the lives of 10 complex individuals, the views of staff and the researcher's personal experiences/knowledge and end up with a cohesive framework for a new understanding of mentorship, was a daunting task — it also required not being overly influenced by the consensus views of mentoring's effectiveness. But what was proven beyond a reasonable doubt — even though mentoring is a positive intervention, it is surely not enough.

The lives of twins Jalen and Justin, siblings Marion and Marshauna, Shaundrel, Marcus, Terrell, Cortez, Jason, and Destiny were far more dynamic than most could have imagined. Their stories helped to answer the primary research questions that guided this study. They had the courage to slightly open up their lives to a stranger. Still, the researcher discovered by comparing their responses to the Program Coordinator's, that some operated with a high level of constraint while others were more candid. The reason that the researcher wanted to incorporate the Program Coordinator's remarks is he could not solely rely on the teen participants to tell their complex stories, which are constantly being edited because of the inherent struggles they endure. So often these kids have opened up only to be left more broken than before. The researcher did not want these kids to be a product of an overzealous scholar who would prick their wounds of despair only to leave them lifeless in his departure. In fact, the researcher intentionally made it clear this research wanted to awaken the voices of at-risk mentees who often are silenced by their pain and to provide some hope to those some consider hopeless.

Research Question One

How can mentor-mentee relationships provide a positive and/or effective alternative for at-risk youth to combat systemic issues like poverty, gun violence, and high dropout rates?

Like most kids, these teens have faith in some caring adults despite being disappointed by family members and countless others. Jalen, Justin, Marion, Marshauna, Shaundrel, Marcus, Terrell, Cortez, Jason, and Destiny enter the Community Youth Center five days a week, carrying emotional baggage heavier than the luggage load on a Boeing 747 — yet although their lives are fraught with extreme turbulence, they continue to fly. They are unaware of the label "at-risk" and even when told, still don't quite understand its implications. They know a community plagued with violence, gunfire, and crime, and some believe that is unlikely to change. Mostly all the teens believed the Community Youth Center, their mentors and caring adults could save them from the circumstances haunting their lives. But unbeknownst to them neither their mentors nor the Community Youth Center can save them all from the systemic cycle of poverty, for its hold on communities like Prairie Urban is too strong. Perhaps with enough resilience, effort, and good luck, a few may make it out, but many will succumb to their environment unless we acknowledge and tackle the true cause of their afflictions — poverty.

The research indicated a need to have stronger parental involvement but within these 10 stories, it did not seem to matter whether the teens were from stable or dysfunctional homes — regardless, they had all descended on the same runway of "at-risk". The researcher is not suggesting increased parental involvement will not render positive outcomes, but it cannot loosen the fatal grip of poverty.

Being visionary, could we possibly impede poverty's grip by simply providing one-on-one mentoring for all at-risk youth? Teens like Shaundrel, Jason, Marion, and Cortez have had positive mentee-mentor relationships for years, but this clearly has not been stronger than the weight of injustice poverty inevitably creates. We know that peer pressure is a force all teens must face irrespective of socio-economic status. In contrast, the influence of peer pressure pails in intensity to the effects of poverty. Teens that have solid grades, no legal infractions, supportive parents, and have demonstrated leadership among their peers, but live in a community ravished by poverty, still have uphill climbs toward opportunity. Poverty is the parent of crime, violence, low achievement, low expectations, and learned helplessness. If we desire to break its cycle, we must make a concerted effort to not target only its offspring.

Research Question Two

How are non-familial relationships like the dyadic relationship of the mentor-mentee perceived from the mentee's perspective?

The research produced another strong endorsement for mentoring. Shaundrel recalled when he and his mentor went fishing and hunting. Many of the teens expressed excitement when their mentor picked them up and took them to lunch or an activity outside of the community. Some have gladly visited the homes of their mentors and have invited them to their homes. Even those teens not yet having had a mentor still believed the mentor-mentee relationship could help them withstand the reality of their circumstances. The staff reflected on their mentor relationships and lent credence to its positive outcomes. The researcher throughout the study drew on his thirty years of experience having positive mentor-mentee relationships. But how are we truly measuring the outcome? Yes, Jalen, Justin, Marion, Marshauna, Shaundrel, Marcus, Terrell, Cortez, Jason, and Destiny all believe in mentoring, but can it truly help them with their struggles? Shaundrel has had a mentor for years but still finds himself in a situation in which graduation from a traditional high school may be unrealistic. Reports derived from census data show median incomes based on academic achievement from no high school diploma to advanced degrees, but we have become more focused on reporting the data than on developing solutions to continually improve the findings. We should move beyond the mere notion of the positive outcomes that mentor-mentee relationships can produce, to the more taxing reality that mentoring alone cannot move the concrete pillars of injustice, which poverty creates causing the most vulnerable populations to be inevitably trapped. How much longer will we blame everyone and everything for the consequences of poverty? How long will we throw our legislative prowess, our economic resources, passions and rhetoric behind something we know will only help a few vulnerable youth? We must not unfairly task nonprofits like the Community Youth Center to contend with a systemic issue in which they did not create nor have the capacity to eradicate. Perhaps we should make a conscious effort to utilize the full weight of justice to overtake the evilness of injustice. It is hard to imagine that Jalen, Justin, Marion, Marshauna, Shaundrel, Marcus, Terrell, Cortez, Jason, and Destiny said when I grow up I want to be a failure. I want to steal. I want to be born into a family that has been generationally dealing with oppression, discrimination, and hopelessness. I want to be a part of a marginalized group. I want someone to shoot me, so I don't have to grow up. I want to live my entire life being labeled and targeted. I want to be at-risk, endangered and destined for failure. I want people to judge me by the color of my skin. I want to go to prison, not college. I want to have a child when I am still a child. And please, I want my future to be based solely on my mentor and community center and not by the Declaration of Independence which states, "All men are created equal, that they are endowed by their Creator with certain unalienable Rights." So the research is clear the mentor-mentee relationship is supported by these 10 teens but when will someone tell them the unfiltered truth. In a matter of time, for some sooner than imagined Jalen, Justin, Marion, Marshauna, Shaundrel, Marcus, Terrell, Cortez, Jason, and Destiny will no longer be between the ages of 13-18 and the doors of the Community Youth Center and high school will close leaving them to scurry along the streets of unfilled dreams and hopes.

The only seemingly opened doors lead to a prison cell or a cemetery entrance. Morally and as a matter of right, we owe it to these kids and all kids born into the sinful, shameful and unapologetic veracity of poverty more options than that....

CHAPTER 6
DISCUSSION, IMPLICATIONS AND CONCLUSION

At the onset of this study, it was evidenced by the robust body of research, that mentoring proves an effective intervention for at-risk youth plagued by systemic issues like poverty, crime, and high dropout rates. Despite the high level of consensus stating mentoring is effective, this study aimed to provide the perspective of the mentees and their lived experiences. One of the most compelling themes this study showcased is that teens who have been labeled at-risk by various systems like schools, legislators, social service agencies and others are completely unaware of their at-risk status. Yes, they acknowledged their communities are violent and rampant with gangs and criminal activity. Some even acknowledged their homes are dysfunctional — but when they heard the label "at-risk", they expressed being offended, feeling targeted and isolated.

The Community Youth Center, like many similar organizations, is committed to doing its part to curtail violence in the community, but its efforts usually fall short because the weight of poverty is too taxing. Irrespective of this reality, the Extend-a-Hand Program provides a safe haven for some of the communities' most vulnerable populations, but once they exit the doors of the Community Youth Center they will be left to fend for themselves. They are in desperate need of more caring adults and as the African proverb instructs, "It takes a village to raise a child." Perhaps the village needs expansion beyond immediate and extended family, community centers and local churches, to be wide enough to reach the moral consciousness and executive and legislative authority of governments to break the cycle of poverty. It is time to destroy the label of at-risk because it only sends a message to our children that they are endangered, targeted and should be on the run. If we can tirelessly fight to save and protect some of our most beloved animals, then surely we can have the courage and tenacity to fight for the most vulnerable human populations within our great nation. Poverty is not a rural or urban problem but is a problem that affects everyone. No mentoring program, let alone a mentor-mentee relationship, has the depth to confront poverty's suffocating nature that turns dreams into horror films and hope into despair. The voices of the teens featured in this study and trapped in the vestiges of poverty should no longer be silenced or ignored. If we are to continue to embrace the positive factors of mentoring programs, we must not divorce ourselves from the reality of cause and effect.

At-risk teens need more than the intervention of mentoring — they desperately need a solution to poverty that unequivocally undermines and limits their chances for a positive future. The potential solutions can include but are not limited to, equal and equitable educational opportunities, gainful employment with livable wages, safe communities void of illicit drugs and crime, and adequate mental health resources. The advantaged manage the former very well for themselves. Also needed are societal changes such as re-imagining a penal system so that it no longer unfairly targets at-risk populations — and restoring the family unit. But the vitriolic nature of poverty very often causes selective amnesia or tonic immobility for the privileged — impeding their potentially significant contributions toward providing solutions for those on the other side of the tracks.

The term "at-risk" is based on a deficit model which inherently limits a person's ability to see others beyond the narrowed focus the term creates. Our ideation must move beyond the label "at-risk" which focuses on things we believe and even know can impede a child's success. We must take a more positive stance, focusing on the individual gifts and talents each child innately possesses. In every facet of our existence no matter how dire the situation, we have the capacity to rise above our circumstances but to be clear, such a possibility is fraught with many obstacles — fear, anxiety, injustice, lack of opportunity, poverty and many more. These may not destroy the child's gifts but at best will make them dormant. When a child speaks for the first time, it is cause for celebration. When that child moves from speaking single words to complete sentences, all are amazed. If that same child begins to play the piano at three years old one might say he or she is gifted and despite their poverty, if that gift is celebrated and continually honed perhaps they can rise above his circumstances.

I was by all accounts at-risk, but my mother checked every homework assignment, insisted I had good penmanship, corrected me when I spoke improperly, examined my attire to ensure it was neat, taught me how to write and once she realized my gifts, she never stopped encouraging me to perfect my talents. Jalen, Justin, Marion, Marshauna, Shaundrel, Marcus, Terrell, Cortez, Jason, and Destiny all have gifts, but all we chose to focus on is their risk factors. Whether on Hollywood Boulevard or Crump Boulevard in Memphis (named the most dangerous neighborhood in America) the commonality among the children is they all have gifts irrespective of their zip code. The label "at-risk" boxes some of the most talented and gifted children in by focusing on their perceived deficits and not their God-given abilities. For some children, school causes great anxiety and can be debilitating but there are countless stories of a child deemed at-risk and unteachable who discovered their gift and rose above those labels. We see this evidenced daily in the entertainment industry. How is it that a child born with sight, loses his vision and in blindness realizes he can play the piano? Someone must have celebrated his gift and not his deficit. That little blind boy, Ray Charles Robinson, grew into a man known as a musical genius and world icon. How about the impoverished family from Gary, Indiana who focused on the gifts of the nine children? The family would become known as the Jacksons and their youngest brother Michael Jackson would become a megastar and given the name King of Pop. And then there is this child abandoned by his father and raised by his grandparents. He too would become a world icon as he broke down the doors of the White House which slaves built to become the first African-American president of the United States of America, Barack Hussein Obama. We must focus on children's gifts and not their at-risk factors that only limit their ability to maximize their talents. We are good at discovering and developing athletes and entertainers, but what about looking beyond risk factors to discover the biochemists that might cure cancer, mathematicians, engineers and the countless others. Mentoring programs cannot see kids only through a deficit lens but must keenly focus on unmasking and awakening the gifts that lie underneath the soot created by the confinement of labels.

One of the unflinching and inarguable facts of this study for Jalen, Justin, Marion, Marshauna, Shaundrel, Marcus, Terrell, Cortez, Jason, and Destiny is that no one has focused on their gifts. All we know are the immense pressures their complex lives entail. Most of the teen participants had no clue they were labeled at-risk and once learned displayed anger but the greater mystery lies in knowing if anyone has highlighted their gifts more than they have focused on their at-risk factors.

Eugene L. Moore, Ph.D.

Implications

This study aims to offer some practical solutions to improve the mentor-mentee relationship. The need to provide one-on-one mentoring, close staffing gaps and rethink how we label youth as at-risk are at the forefront of feasible implications. Having sat down with 10 teens ranging from 13-18 years of age, observing their interactions and getting an in depth look into their case files, has deeply informed how the mentor-mentee relationship is understood. All of these teens were lumped into a single category, "at-risk", yet their risk factors ranged from extreme poverty to infractions with the law. The only factor with complete commonality was their daily participation in the Extend-a-Hand Program. They believed the Community Youth Center has the capacity to prevent them from being engaged in dangerous activities like violence and crime after-school but they are seemingly unaware of the systemic issue of poverty which helps perpetuate crime and violence.

As mentioned in the findings, the Program Coordinator stated the teens need more individualized support and the center cannot truly account for those hours during which the teens are not in their care. The Community Youth Center definitely needs a facility upgrade but even if it was increased by 50,000 square feet, this would not fill the need for highly trained mentors to provide one-to-one mentoring. In order for mentoring programs to have success, it is imperative they secure mentors who are capable of providing frequent interaction in an effort to create a sustainable relationship with their mentees (Miller, J., Barnes, Miller, H., & McKinnon, 2012). It is apparent the participants of the Extend-a-Hand Program are largely attracted to playing basketball, especially since the center decided to form a basketball team featuring the Extend-a-Hand Program participants. But the allure of basketball does not negate yearning needs for caring adults. The findings suggested the desire to spend more time with their mentors like going to lunch and taking trips outside the neighborhood were highly positive factors of their mentor-mentee experience. It is important not only to have a deep pool of quality mentors but also equally important to have a stable staff — far too often as soon as a student begins to trust a mentor or a staff member, that person leaves the organization.

In the recent past, the Community Youth Center experienced some extreme financial issues almost resulting in its closure. It has rebounded somewhat but staffing woes continue to plague the center. Like most non-profits providing social services, compensation for workers is very low — despite the intensely demanding nature of the work and long days often extending beyond scheduled hours. In schools, due to constraints of the classroom, teachers lack the capacity to provide the critical care needed to assist some of their most vulnerable students — redoubling the importance of caring, adult staff in youth centers. Although after-school programs have various types of programming and mentoring staff can provide a consistent caring adult to the at-risk population, funding often impedes those opportunities (Rhodes, 2004). During the time frame of this study, the Community Youth Center lost several volunteers and a staff member who had developed a strong multi-year bond with the members. Losing staff and volunteers creates mistrust, sometimes even deterring members from trying to develop deep attachments for fear of abandonment again as they have experienced in the past. Besides the mistrust created from mentor and staff inconsistency, the label of "at-risk" also produces a level of anxiety for teens — as one teen eloquently expressed, it made her feel as if someone was watching her.

The term "at-risk" has come to mean a variety of risk factors —

single-parent homes, substance abuse, low-income, school delinquency, criminal infractions, and others. But while this label allows researchers, schools legislators, and countless others to neatly define and categorize youth, it is truly not fully understood by the very population it hopes to protect. There is limited to no research on the term itself other than defining its catch-all meaning. It seems we all would be better served if we eliminated the term. There was a consensus from all the teen participants, the researcher, and the staff members — these teens were unaware of their at-risk factors and status. Labels are tricky. Some believe awareness of being at-risk places you in greater danger because it can create paranoia and hopelessness. This is evidenced in the teens featured in this study — all had seemed clueless of their at-risk status, but learning of their status only conjured negative feelings. If systemic issues like poverty and discrimination — all increasing the probability of crime, violence, high dropout rates, low-income, substance abuse, and future single-parent homes — were eliminated, what would become of this readily used term "at-risk"?

Limitations of this Study

All research studies, no matter how meticulously presented and designed, will have inherent limitations. Hence, this study is no different and presents a few notable limitations. First, the age of the participants ranged from 13-18 years of age which made the depth of the responses to the interview questions varied despite presenting some common themes. Some of the interviewees had only had one experience with mentoring compared to some participants who had multiple or extended experiences. Furthermore, their lived experiences were grossly different from each other — consider Terrell, who at only 15 years of age already had a 1 year old son. During the study, the Extend-a-Hand Program was 73% male and 27% female; the participant pool, 80% and 20% male and female respectively. A limitation was that the two females in the study were only 13 and 14 years of age, effectively excluding older females from referral by the two participants. However, according to the Program Coordinator, some older girls were not featured in the study because of sporadic attendance, frequently going weeks at a time without visits to the center.

Secondly, the time allowed to complete the study proved to be a limitation as potential participants were frequently absent during the interviewing phase of the study. Even during the observation, it was apparent that some members were absent for days at a time without staff member awareness of their status as they would simultaneously miss school. The staff would reach out to the parent or guardian to seek information about the participant's whereabouts but more often than not could not account for the disappearances. Thus, if more time had been available more voices may have possibly been incorporated in the study.

Also, the sampling method presented a limitation if the featured participants referred only prospective participants they believed had similar backgrounds to their own. However, the study featured both fraternal twins and other siblings — it became immediately obvious that participants had their own unique lived experiences and appeared honest and sincere as they engaged the questions. To minimize possible limitations of the sampling method, participants were given some key expectations for potential participants, coupled with detailed information from the staff case management, provided by the Program Coordinator.

Finally, the researcher was careful to document his previous experience with organizations like the Community Youth Center and programs similar to Extend-a-Hand that could have unintentionally presented some bias in the findings. The researcher took concrete steps to avoid bias — first by allowing the participants to fully disclose their responses without any hindrance. Further, the researcher was fully cognizant of the participants' tone, body language, and other non-verbal cues. Together these ensured complete transparency. The researcher contends that while his previous experiences of being a mentee and a mentor were positive, his personal experiences had little to no bearing on the findings of this study. Rather the researcher's approach was thorough and open-minded to objectively glean from the participants' interviews, their fully-intended communications.

Directions for Future Research

This study intentionally veered away from focusing on the effectiveness of mentoring as an intervention for at-risk youths; rather it explored the mentor-mentee relationship through the lens of teens participating in an after-school program. However, more research into how programs are designed, how success is measured and how success helps alleviate other precursor problems — allowing similar interventions to be applied to poverty, crime, and high dropout rates. The study spoke directly to the primary benefactor of the intervention, the mentee, but more research is needed to deeply understand the role of the parent or guardian. In this study, we learned about siblings who experienced extreme abuse from their father and although their relationship with their father has improved, their mother chastises them for poor choices and scars of abuse are still present. Having deeper understanding from parents about their upbringing would bring some needed context as to why their children are deemed at-risk. It is equally important to understand who, outside of the parent and mentor, is an example of a caring adult — teachers, clergy, extended family and community organizations — because future research needs to unpack these relationships and see how they are defining at-risk teens. The center's staff has mostly defined youth by their risk factors — future research needs to explore how these categorizations affect those it aims to protect and serve. In fact, are caring adults consciously or subconsciously boxing children in by their labels or looking past the labels to provide a meaningful plan for the future? Such an analysis would provide an understanding of what effects these labels are truly having on children and if they are doing more harm than good. The study revealed that the Extend-a-Hand Program serves as a last-ditch effort to intervene in the lives of at-risk teens — more research needs to be conducted to discover how the mentor-mentee relationship can serve as a preventative measure for vulnerable populations.

Lastly, it is vital that future research incorporates the tenets of Critical Race Theory (CRT) as it would likely provide a deeper analysis and understanding of the labels assigned to at-risk African-Americans — more than likely heavily correlated to the pervasiveness of racism in American society. The systemic cycle of poverty is largely supported by power structures that perpetuate discrimination, oppression, and marginalization of African-Americans. Thus, CRT could provide a critical lens as to why mentoring programs have become a readily used intervention for African-Americans and perhaps provide context explaining why the intervention alone cannot dismantle power structures which inevitably rebirth and continue the cycle of poverty.

Closing Remarks

On the Run

As a kid, I had no worries or concern
As a kid, my only job was to learn

As a kid, I watched my mother work with no indication of a struggle
As a kid, my life was in a protective and nurturing bubble

As a kid, I had no idea what my mom was protecting me from
As a kid, I had no clue I was a target and should be on the run

As a teen, I had to run even faster for the chase had become intense
As a teen, I started to realize the system for years had labeled me at-risk

At-risk for dropping out of school
At-risk because I did not follow all the rules
At-risk because of the violence in my community
At-risk because of my father's absence and failure to take responsibility
At-risk because of gangs, drugs and high dropout rates
At-risk because like all people I made a few mistakes
At-risk because of my low-income and likelihood to go to prison
At-risk because having a child as a child would likely be my decision

Mentors Matter But Poverty Sucks

At-risk because I was told I had ADHD and quickly given an IEP

Now as an adult, I realize these systems have always been targeting me

As an adult, I still have to keep watch because even if I receive an advanced degree

The system will always try to challenge, delegitimize and target me

Not because I am deficient or less than

But because I have never followed their plan

A plan that puts poverty in your midst, where only a few make it out

So you see poverty is what truly makes failure come about

Labels are distracting and can box you in

Forcing you to run a race which some hope you never win

So run as fast as you can and make sure you simply have fun

I encourage you to be resilient even when you are on the run.

Eugene L. Moore, Ph.D.

References

Abbaly, J. (2011). Mentoring Youths: Key to Unlocking the Future. *IFE PsychologIA*, No. 1, pp. 156-168.

Alexander, M. (2012). *The New Jim Crow: Mass Incarceration in the Age of Colorblindness*, The New Press.

Allen, T., Eby, L., & Lentz, E. (2006). Mentoring Behaviors and Mentoring Quality Associated with Formal Mentoring Programs: Closing the Gap Between Research and Practice. *Journal of Applied Psychology*, Vol. 91, No. 3, pp. 567-578.

Amato, P. R., Patterson, S., Beattie, B. (2015). Single-parent Households and Children's Educational Achievement: A State-level Analysis, *Social Science Research*, Vol. 53, pp. 191-202.

Anda, D. (2001). A Qualitative Evaluation of a Mentor Program for At-Risk Youth: The Participant' Perspective. *Child and Adolescent Social Work Journal*, Vol. 18, No. 2, pp.97-117.

Anastasia, T., Skinner, R., & Mundhenk, S. (2012). Youth Mentoring: Program and Mentor Best Practices. *Journal of Family & Consumer Sciences*, Vol. 104, No. 2, pp.38-44.

Belgrave, L., & Charmaz, K. (2012). Qualitative Interviewing and Grounded Theory Analysis. In Jaber F. Gubrium, James A. Holstein, Amir B. Marvasti, & Karyn D.McKinney (Eds.), The SAGE Handbook of Interview Research: The Complexity of the Craft. (2nd ed., pp. 347-367). Thousand Oaks, CA: SAGE Publications.

Bellamy, N. D., Sale, E., Wang, M. Q., Springer, J. F., & Rath Susie. (2006). Spoken, but Perhaps not Heard; Youth Perceptions on the Relationship with their Adult Mentors. *Journal of Youth Ministry*, Vol. 5, No. 1, pp. 57-75.

Biggs S., Musewe, L., Harvey, J. (2014). Mentoring and Academic Performance of Black and Under-Resourced Urban Middle Grade Students. *The Negro Educational Review*, Vol. 65, No. 1-4, pp.64-86.

Blake-Beard, S., Bayne, M., Crosby, F., & Muller, C. (2011). Matching by Race and Gender in Mentoring Relationships: Keeping our Eyes on the Prize.*Journal of Social Issues*, Vol. 67, No. 3, pp.622-643.

Blakeslee, J., & Keller, T. (2012). Building the Youth Mentoring Knowledge Base: Publishing Trends and Coauthorship Networks. *Journal of Community Psychology*, Vol. 40, No. 7, pp.845-859.

Boundless (2016). Boundless Sociology. Retrieved from https://www.boundless.com/sociology/textbooks/boundless-sociology-textbook/sociology-1/theoretical-perspectives-in-sociology-24/the-symbolic-interactionist-perspective-157-3185/

Bowers, E., Johnson, S., Buckingham, M., Gasca, S., Warren, D., Lerner, J., & Lerner R. (2014). Important Non-parental Adults and Positive Youth Development across Mid-to-Late-Adolescence: The Moderating Effect of Parenting Profiles. *J Youth Adolescence*, Vol. 43, pp. 897-918.

Brink, P.J. and Wood, M.J. (1989). *Advanced Design in Nursing Research*. Thousand Oaks, CA: Sage Publications, Inc.

Britner, P.A., Balcazar, F. E., Blechman, E. A., Blinn-Pike, L., & Larose S. (2006). Mentoring Special Youth Populations, *Journal of Community Psychology*, Vol. 34, No. 6, pp. 747-763.

Broussard, C., Mosley-Howard, S., & Roychoudhury, A. (2006). Using Youth Advocates for Mentoring At-Risk Students in Urban Settings. *Children & Schools*, Vol. 28, No. 2, pp.122-127.

Brown, W. (2006). Resiliency and the Mentoring Factor. *Reclaiming Children and Youth*, Vol. 13, No. 2, pp.75-79.

Bulanda, J. J., & McCrea, K. T. (2013). The Promise of an Accumulation of Care: Disadvantaged African-American Youths' Perspectives about What Makes an After School Program Meaningful. *Child and Adolescence Social Work Journal*, No.30, pp. 95-118.

Bush, L. (2005). Helping America's Youth. *Reclaiming Children and Youth*, Vol. 14, No. 2, pp.69-70.

Chenitz, C. and Swanson, C. (1986). *From Practice to Grounded Theory: Qualitative Research in Nursing*, Menlo Park, CA: Addison-Wesley.

Christiansen, J., Christiansen, J. L., & Howard, M. (1997). Using Protective Factors to Enhance Resilience and School Success for At-Risk Students. *Intervention in School and Clinic*, Vol. 33, No. 2, pp.86-89.

Colman, R., & Colman, A. (2003). A National Roundup of Recent Press Reports on Youth Issues. *Youth Studies Australia*, Vol. 22, No. 2, pp. 3-10.

Converse, N., & Lignugaris/Kraft, B. (2009). Evaluation of a School-based Mentoring Program for At-Risk Middle School Youth. *Remedial and Special Education*, Vol. 30, No. 33, pp.33-46.

Corbin, J. & Strauss, A. (1990). *Basics of Qualitative Research: Grounded Theory Procedures and Techniques.* New Park, CA: Sage Publications.

Corbin, J. & Strauss, A. (1998). *Basics of Qualitative Research Techniques and Procedures for Developing Grounded Theory.* London, UK: Sage Publications, Inc.

Corbin, J. & Strauss, A. (2015). *Basics of Qualitative Research Techniques and Procedures for Developing Grounded Theory.* Fourth Edition. Thousand Oaks, CA: Sage Publications, Inc.

Dahlvig, J. (2010). Mentoring of African-American Students at a Predominately White Institution (PWI), *Christian Higher Education*, Vol. 9, pp.369-395.

Darensbourg, A., Perez, E., & Blake, J. J. (2010). Overrepresentation of African American Males in Exclusionary Discipline: The Role of School-Based Mental Health Professionals in Dismantling the School to Prison Pipeline, *Journal of African-American Males in Education*, Vol. 1, No. 3, pp.196-211.

Darling, N., Bogat, G., Cavell, T., Murphy, S., & Sanchez, B. (2006). Gender, Ethnicity, Development, and Risk: Mentoring and the Consideration of Individual Differences. *Journal of Community Psychology*, Vol. 34, No. 6, pp.765-779.

Dawson, K. (2009). Principles of Academic Success and Mentorship: An Interview with Saundra McGuire. *Journal of Developmental Education*, Vol. 33, No. 2, pp.22-25.

Day, A. (2006). The Power of Social Support: Mentoring and Resilience. *Reclaiming Children and Youth*, Vol. 14, No. 4, pp.196-198.

Denson-Smith, G. L. (2007). Adolescent Black Males Living in Poverty: Perceived Sense of Inadequacy, Relations with Parents and their Relationship with Attitudes to School and Attitudes to Teachers (Doctoral dissertation). Retrieved from ProQuest Information and Learning Company. (UMI No. 3274600).

Deutsch, N., & Spencer, R. (2009). Capturing the Magic: Assessing the Quality of Youth Mentoring Relationships. *New Directions for Youth Development*, Vol. 121, pp. 47-70.

Dey I. (1999). *Grounding Grounded Theory: Guidelines for Qualitative Inquiry.* San Diego, CA: Academic Press.

DuBois, D. L., Doolittle, F., Yates, B. T., Silverthorn, N., & Tebes, J. K. (2006). Research Methodology and Youth Mentoring. *Journal of Community Psychology*, Vol. 34, No. 6, pp. 657-676.

DuBois, D. L., Neville, H. A., Parra, G. R., & Pugh-Lilly, A. O. (2002). Testing a New Model of Mentoring. *New Directions for Youth Development*, Spring, No. 93, pp. 21-57.

DuBois, D. L., Portillo, N., Rhodes, J.E., Silverthorn, N., & Valentine, J. C. (2011). How Effective are Mentoring Programs for Youth? A Systematic Assessment of the Evidence. *Association for Psychological Science in the Public Interest*, Vol. 12, No. 2, pp. 57-91.

DuBois, D. L., & Silverthorn, N. (2005). Natural Mentoring Relationships and Adolescent Health: Evidence from a National Study. *American Journal of Public Health*, Vol. 95, No. 3, pp. 518-524.

Durlak, J. A. (2011). Are Mentoring Programs a Worthwhile Social Investment? *Psychological Science in the Public Interest.* Vol. 12, No. 2, pp. 55-56.

Empey, C., Riggs, K., & Lee, T. R. (2002). Mentoring as a Prevention Strategy: A Promising Program in Utah. *Journal of Family & Consumer Sciences*, Vol. 94, No.4, pp. 75-76.

Flick, U. (Eds.) (2009). *An Introduction to Qualitative Research: Uwe Flick*. London: Sage Publications.

Flick, U., Kardorff, E., & Steinke, I. (Eds.) (2004) *A Companion to Qualitative Research*. London: Sage Publications.

Fraenkel, J. & Wallen, N. (2011). *How to Design and Evaluate Research in Education*. New York: McGraw Hill.

Freedman, M. (1991). The Kindness of Strangers: Reflections on the Mentoring Movement, Public/Private Ventures. Philadelphia, PA: Public/Private Ventures. (ERIC Document Reproduction Service No. ED341749).

Frey, L., Botan, C., & Kreps, G. (2000). *Investigating Communication: An Introduction to Research Methods*, 2nd ed. Boston: Allyn and Bacon.

Friedman, H. (2013). *Playing to Win Raising Children in a Competitive Culture*. Los Angeles: University of California Press

Fruiht, V., & Wray-Lake, E. (2013). The Role of Mentor Type and Timing in Predicting Educational Attainment. *Journal of Youth and Adolescence*, Vol. 42, pp. 1459-1472.

Fuller, R. D., Percy, V. E., Bruening, J. E., & Cotrufo, R. J. (2013). Positive Youth Development: Minority Male Participation in Sport-Based after-school Program in an Urban Environment. *Research Quarterly for Exercise and Sport*, Vol. 84, No. 4, pp. 469-482.

Gil, D. (2013). *Confronting Injustice and Oppression Concepts and Strategies for Social Workers*. New York: Columbia University Press.

Glaser B. & Strauss A. (1967). *The Discovery of Grounded Theory: Strategies for Qualitative Research*. New York: Aldine de Gruyter.

Greene, K., Lee, B., Constance, N. & Hynes, K. (2013). Examining Youth and Program Predictors of Engagement in Out-of-School Time Programs. *J Youth Adolescence*, Vol. 42, pp. 1557-1572.

Grineski, S. (2003). A University and Community-Based Partnership: After-School Mentoring Mentoring for Low-Income Youth. *School Community Journal*, Vol. 13, No. 1, pp. 101-114.

Grossman, J., & Rhodes, J. (2002). The Test of Time: Predictors and Effects of Duration in Youth Mentoring Relationships. *American Journal of Communication*, Vol. 30, No. 2, pp. 199-219.

Hall. H. (2015). Food for Thought: Using Critical Pedagogy in Mentoring African-American Adolescent Males. *The Black Scholar*, Vol. 45, No. 3, pp. 39-53.

Hamilton, S., Hamilton, M. A., Hirsh, B. J., Hughes, J., King, J., & Kenneth, M. (2006). Community Contexts for Mentoring, *Journal of Community Psychology*, Vol. 34, No. 6, pp. 727-746.

Hamilton, S., & Hamilton, M. A . (2010). Building Mentoring Relationships. *New Directions for Youth Development*, No. 126, pp. 141-144.

Hanson, K., Guilfoy, V., & Pillai, S. (2009). *More than Title IX: How Equity in Education has Shaped the Nation*, Lanham, MD: Rowman & Littlefield Publishers, Inc.

Hartley, R. (2004). Young People and Mentoring, *Family Matters*, Winter No. 68, pp. 22-27.

Hendricks, V. M., Blanken, P. and Adriaans, N. (1992). *Snowball Sampling: Pilot Study on Cocaine Use*, Rotterdam, Netherlands: IVOL.

Herrera, C., DuBois, D. L., Grossman, J. B., Public/Private Ventures, MDRC, & Bill and Melinda Gates Foundation (2013). The Role of Risk: Mentoring Experiences and Outcomes for Youth with Varying Risk Profiles. New York, NY: A Public/Private Ventures project distributed by MDRC.

Higginbotham, B., MacArthur, S., & Dart, P. (2010). 4-H Mentoring: Youth and Families with Promise—Adult Engagement and Development of Strengths in Youth. *Journal of Prevention & Intervention in the Community*, Vol. 38, No. 3, pp. 229-243.

Holt, L., Bry, B., & Johnson, V. (2008). Enhancing School Engagement in At-Risk, Urban Minority Adolescents through a School-Based, Adult Mentoring Intervention. *Child & Family Behavior*, Vol. 30, No. 4, pp.297-318.

Hughes, C., & Dykstra, S. J. (2008). University Students' Expectations for Mentoring High-Poverty Youth. *Journal of Community Engagement and Scholarship*, Vol. 1, No. 1, pp. 21-32.

Institution for Urban and Minority Education (IUME). (1992). Evaluating Mentoring Programs, *IMUE*, No. 1, pp 3-6.

Jackson, K.B. (2003). From Sand to Cement: Understanding the Big Brothers Big Sisters School Buddies Program in Champaign-Urbana (Unpublished doctoral dissertation). University of Illinois at Urbana-Champaign Urbana, Illinois.

Jekielek, S., Moore, K. A., & Hair, E. C. (2002). Mentoring Programs and Youth Development, Washington, DC: Child Trends. (ERIC Document Reproduction Service No. ED465457).

Johnson, W. (2007). *On Being a Mentor a Guide for Higher Education Faculty*. Mahwah, NJ: Lawrence Erlbaum Associates, Publishers.

Johnson, W., Rich, L., & Keene, L. (2016). Father-Son Communication: An Intervention Strategy for Boys and Men of Color to Promote Neighborhood Safety Post-Ferguson. *Journal of Men's Studies*, Vol. 24, No. 2, pp. 151-165.

Kanchewa, S., Rhodes, J., Schwartz, S., & Olsho, L. (2014). An Investigation of Same- Versus Cross-gender Matching for Boys in Formal School-based Mentoring Programs. *Applied Developmental Science*, Vol. 18, No. 1, pp. 31-45.

Karcher, M. J., Herrera, C., & Hansen, K. (2010). "I dunno, what do you wanna do?" Testing a Framework to Guide Mentor Training and Activity Selection. *New Direction for Youth Development*, Summer, No. 126, pp. 69.

Karcher, M. J. & Nakkula, M. J. (2010). Youth Mentoring with a Balanced Focus, Shared Purpose, and Collaborative Interactions. *New Directions for Youth Development*, Summer, No. 126, pp. 13-32.

Karcher, M., Kuperminc, G., Portwood, S., Sipe, C., & Taylor, A. (2006). Mentoring Programs: A Framework to Inform Program Development, Research, and Evaluation. *Journal of Community Psychology*, Vol. 34, No. 6, pp. 709-725.

Keating, L., Tomishima, M., Foster, S., & Alessandri, M, (2002). The Effects of a Mentoring Program on At-risk Youth. *Adolescence*, Vol. 37, No. 148, pp. 717-734.

Keller, T. E., & Pryce, J. (2010). Mutual but Unequal: Mentoring as a Hybrid of Familiar Relationship Roles. *New Directions for Youth Development*, No. 126, pp. 33-50.

King, N., & Horrocks, C. (2010). *Interviews in Qualitative Research*. Los Angeles: SAGE Research Methods

Komosa-Hawkins. (2010). Best Practices in School-Based Mentoring Programs for Adolescents. *Child & Youth Services*, No. 31, pp. 121-137.

Kvale, S. (1996). *Interviews: An Introduction to Qualitative Research Interviewing*. Thousand Oaks, CA: Sage Publications.

Lakind, D., Eddy, M., & Zell, A. (2014). Mentoring Youth at High Risk: The Perspectives of Professional Mentors. *Child Youth Care Forum*, Vol. 43, pp.705-727.

Langhout, R., Rhodes, J., & Osborne, L. (2004). An Exploratory Study of Youth Mentoring in an Urban Context: Adolescents' Perceptions of Relationship Styles. *Journal of Youth and Adolescence*, Vol. 33, No. 4, pp.293-306.

Larose, S., DeWit, D., Lipman, E. & DuBois, D. (2004). The Role of Relational, Recreational, and Tutoring Activities in the Perceptions of Received Support and Quality of Mentoring Relationship during a Community-Based Mentoring Relationship. *Journal of Community Psychology*, Vol. 43, No. 5, pp.527-544.

Lee, J., Germain, L., Lawerence, C., & Marshall, J. (2010). "It Opened My Mind My Eyes, It Was Good". Supporting College Students' Navigation of Difference in a Youth Mentoring Program. *Educational Horizons*, Vol. 89, No. 1, pp.33-46.

Lee, K., Kim, M., Park, T., & Alcazar-Bejerano, I. (2015). Effects of a Ubiquitous Mentoring Program on Self-Esteem, School Adaptation, and Perceived Parental Attitude.*Society for Personality Research*, Vol. 43, No. 7, pp. 1193-1208.

Levine, A. & Dean, D. (2012). *Generation on a Tightrope*. San Francisco: Jossey-Bass.

Leyton-Armakan, J., Lawrence, E., Deutsch, N., Williams, J., & Henneberger, A. (2012). Effective Youth Mentors: The Relationship between Initial Characteristics of College Women Mentors and Mentee Satisfaction and Outcome. *Journal of Community Psychology*, Vol. 40, No. 8, pp. 906-920.

Liang, B. & Rhodes, J. (2007). Guest Editorial: Cultivating the Vital Element of Youth Mentoring. *Applied Developmental Science*, Vol. 11, No. 2, pp. 104-107.

Mallett, C. (2012). The School Success Program: Improving Maltreated Children's Academic and School-related Outcomes. *Children & Schools*, Vol. 34, No. 1, pp. 13-26.

Mano, M. (2007). Role of Intergenerational Mentoring for Supporting Youth Development: An Examination of the "Across Ages" Program in the U.S. Educational Studies in Japan. *International Yearbook*, No. 2, pp.83-94.

McCluskey, K., Noller, R., Lamoureux, K., & McCluskey, A. (2004). Unlocking Hidden Potential through Mentoring. *Reclaiming Children and Youth*, Vol. 13, No. 2, pp.85-93.

McIntyre, D. & Hagger, H. (Eds). (1996). *Mentors in Schools Developing the Profession of Teaching.* London: David Fulton Publishers.

McKay, C. (2011). The Resilient Community: Implications for Out of School Programming, *Child Adolescence Social Work*, Vol. 28, pp. 357-373.

McLaughlin, C. (2010). Mentoring: What Is It? How Do We Do It and How Do We Get More of It?.*Health Services Research*, Vol. 45, No. 3, pp. 871-884.

McRoy, R. G., & Griffin, A. J. (2015). Family Matters: Strengthening the Fabric of MinorityFamilies. In R. Bangs & L. Davis (Eds.) *Race and Social Problems* (pp. 163-170). Springer: New York.

Meyer, K., & Bouchey, H. (2010). Daring to DREAM: Results from a Mentoring Programme for At-Risk Youth. *International Journal of Evidence Based Coaching and Mentoring*, Vol. 8, No. 1, pp.67-84.

Miller, J., Barnes, J., Miller, H., & McKinnon, L. (2012). Exploring the Link between Mentoring Program Structure & Success Rates: Results from a National Survey. *American Journal of Criminal Justice*, Vol. 38, No. 439, pp.439-459.

Miller, K. (2007). The Benefits of Out-of-School Time Programs. *Principal's Research Review*, Vol. 2, pp. 1-6.

Mitchell, M. L. (2013). National Cares Mentoring Movement. *Reclaiming Children and Youth*, Vol. 22, No. 1, pp. 30-34.

Moodie, M. & Fisher, J. (2009). Are Youth Mentoring Programs Good Value-For-Money? An Evaluation of the Big Brothers Big Sisters Melbourne Program. *BMC Public Health*, Vol. 9, No. 41, pp.1-9.

Mullen, C., Cox, M., Boettcher, A. & Adoue, D. (Eds). (1997). Breaking the Circle of One: Redefining Mentorship in the Lives and Writings of Educators. In G. Webb-Johnson, *My Emerging Destiny: Mentoring from an African-American Perspective.* (2nd ed., pp. 3-19). New York: Peter Lang Publishing, Inc.

Nakkula, M. J., & Harris, J. T. (2010). Beyond the Dichotomy of Work and Fun: Measuring the Thorough Interrelatedness of Structure and Quality in Youth Mentoring Relationships. *New Directions for Youth Development*, Summer, No. 126, pp. 71-87.

Newman, T. (2002). *Promoting Resilience: A Review of Effective Strategies for Child Care Services*, Exeter, United Kingdom: Center for Evidence Based Social Sciences.

Noam, G., Warner, L., & Dyken, L. (2001). Beyond the Rhetoric of Zero Tolerance: Long-term Solutions for At-risk Youth. *New Directions for Youth Development*, No. 92, pp. 155-182.

Ogbu, J. U., & Wilson J. (1990). Mentoring Minority Youth: A Framework, New York, NY: Institute for Urban and Minority Education. (ERIC Document Reproduction Service No. ED354293).

Padgett, D. (2008). *Qualitative Methods in Social Work Research* (2nd ed.). Thousand Oaks, CA: Sage.

Parra, G. R., DuBois, D.L., Neville, H.A., & Pugh-Lilly, A. O. (2002). Mentoring Relationships for Youth: Investigation of a Process-Oriented Model. *Journal of Community Psychology*, Vol. 30, No. 4, pp. 367-388.

Paslay, C. (2011). *The Village Proposal*. Lanham, MD: Rowman & Littlefield Publishers, Inc.

Pedersen, P. J., Woolum, S., Gagne, B., Coleman, M. (2009). Beyond the Norm: Extraordinary Relationships in Youth Mentoring. *Children and Youth Services Review*, No. 31, pp. 1307-1313.

Philip, K. & Hendry, L. (2000). Making Sense of Mentoring or Mentoring Making Sense? Reflections the Mentoring Process by Adult Mentors with Young People. *Journal of Community &Applied Social Psychology*, Vol. 10, pp.211-223.

Powell, B. (2002). The Effects of Development Mentoring on Connectedness and Academic Achievement. *School Community Journal*, Vol. 12, No. 2, pp.35-50.

Pryce, J. (2012). Mentor Attunement: An Approach to Successful School-based Mentoring Relationships. *Child & Adolescent Social Work Journal*, Vol. 29, pp. 285-305.

Randolph, K., & Johnson, J. (2008). School-Based Mentoring Programs: A Review of the Research. *Children & Schools*, Vol. 30, No. 1, pp.177-185.

Ranis, S. (2001). The Rosen Scholars Program: A new Design for Mentoring Disadvantaged Youth for Postsecondary Success Evaluation Summary, ERIC Document Reproduction Service No. ED 451789

Reclaiming Children and Youth (2005). Mentoring the Least of These: An Interview with Duncan Campbell, Vol. 12, No. 2, pp. 91-92.

Renick, N. R., & Zand, D. H. (2009). Mentees' Perceptions of Their Interpersonal Relationships: The Role of the Mentor-Youth Bond. *Youth and Society*, Vol. 41, No. 3, pp. 434-445.

Rhodes, J. (2004). The Critical Ingredient: Caring Youth-Staff Relationships in After-School Settings. *New Directions for Youth Development*, Spring, Vol. 2004, issue. 101, pp. 145-161.

Rhodes, J. (2008). Improving Youth Mentoring Interventions through Research-Based Practice. *American Journal of Community Psychology*, Vol. 41, pp. 35-42.

Rhodes, J. (2002). *Stand by Me: The Risks and Rewards of Mentoring Today's Youth*. Massachusetts: Harvard University Press.

Rhodes, J. E., Liang, B., & Spencer, R. (2009). First Do No Harm: Ethical Principles for Youth Mentoring Relationships. *Professional Psychology: Research and Practice*, Vol. 40, No. 5, pp. 452-458.

Rhodes, J. E., & Chan, C. (2008). Youth Mentoring and Spiritual Development. *New Directions for Youth Development*, Summer, No. 118, pp. 85-89.

Rhodes, J., & Spencer, R. (2010). Structuring Mentorship Relationships for Competence, Character, and Purpose. *New Directions for Youth Development*, Vol. 126, pp. 149-152.

Rhodes, J., & DuBois, D. (2008). Mentoring Relationships and Programs for Youth. *Current Directions in Psychological Science*, Vol. 17, No. 4, pp. 254-258.

Rhodes, J., & DuBois, D. (2006). Understanding and Facilitating the Youth Movement. *Society for Research in Child Development*, Vol. 20, No. 3, pp. 1-20.

Rhodes, J., Grossman, J. B., & Roffman, J. (2002). The Rhetoric and Reality of Youth Mentoring. *New Directions for Youth Development*, Spring, Vol. 93, pp. 9-20.

Rhodes, J. E., Spencer, R., Keller, T. E., Liang, B., & Noam, G. (2006). A Model for the Influence of Mentoring Relationships on Youth Development. *Journal of Community Psychology*, Vol. 34, No. 6, pp. 691-707.

Roberts, D., Johnson, G. S., & Richardson, N. L. (2012). Environmental Justice and Youth of Color at the West Care Foundation in Atlanta, Georgia. *Race, Gender & Class*, Vol. 19, No. 1-2, pp. 192-217.

Royse, D. (1998). Mentoring High-Risk Minority Youth: Evaluation of the Brothers Project. *Adolescence*, Vol. 33, No. 129, pp.145-158.

Schwartz, S. E. O., Rhodes, J.E, Spencer, R., & Grossman, J. (2013). Youth Initiated Mentoring: Investing a New Approach to Working with Vulnerable Adolescents. *American Journal Community Psychology*, Vol. 52, pp. 155-169.

Sealey-Ruiz, Y., & Greene, P. (2010). Embracing Urban Youth Culture in the Context of Education. *Urban Review*, Vol. 43, pp. 339-357.

Shepard, J. (2009). Campus Kids Mentoring Program. *Reclaiming Children and Youth*, Vol. 18, No.3, pp.38-43.

Silverman, D. (2014). *Interpreting Qualitative Data* (5th ed.). Thousand Oaks, CA: Sage.

Spencer, R. (2007). "It's Not What I Expected" A Qualitative Study of Mentoring Relationship Failures. *Journal of Adolescent Research*, Vol. 22, No. 4, pp. 331-354.

Spencer, R. (2006). Understanding the Mentoring Process between Adolescents and Adults. *Youth and Society*, Vol. 37, No. 3, pp. 287-315.

Spencer, R., Basualdo-Delmonico, A., & Lewis, T. O. (2011). Working to Make it Work: The Roles of Parents in Youth Mentoring Process. *Journal of Community Psychology*, Vol. 39, No. 1, pp. 51-59.

Strauss, A., & Corbin, J. (1998). *Basics of Qualitative Research Techniques and Procedures for Developing Grounded Theory* (2nd ed.). Thousand Oaks, London: Sage.

Struchen, W., & Porta, M. (1997). From Role-Modeling to Mentoring for African-American Youth: Ingredients for Successful Relationships. *Preventing School Failure*, Vol. 41, No. 3, pp. 119-123.

Stumbo, N., Blegen, A., & Lindahl-Lewis, P. (2008). Two Mentorship Case Studies of High School and University Students with Disabilities: Milestones and Lessons. *Journal of Rehabilitation*, Vol. 74, No. 2, pp. 45-51.

Taylor, M. E. (2014). Combating Poverty within the Black Community: Conservative Policy Initiatives Hold Potential Solutions. *Harvard Journal of African-American Public Policy*, Vol. 1, No. 1, pp. 5-10.

Townsel, K. T. (1997). Mentoring African-American Youth. *Preventing School Failure: Alternative Education for Children and Youth*, Vol. 41, No. 3, pp. 125-127.

Travis, R. (2010). What They Think: Attribution Made by Youth Workers about Youth Circumstances and the Implications for Service-Delivery in Out-of-School Time Programs. *Child Youth Care Forum*, No. 39, pp. 443-464.

Tully, F. (2004). Mentoring: My Outstanding Teacher of the Year. *Reclaiming Children & Youth*, Vol. 13, No. 2, pp. 68-74.

VanderVen, K. (2004). Adults are Still Needed! Intergenerational and Mentoring Activities. *Reclaiming Children and Youth*, Vol. 13, No. 2, pp.94-102.

Wandersman, A., Clary, E., Forbush, J., Weinberger, S., Coyne, M. and Duffy, J. (2006). Community Organizing and Advocacy: Increasing the Quality and Quantity of Mentoring Programs. *Journal of Community Psychology*, Vol. 34, No. 6, pp.781-799.

Washington, G., Barnes, D., & Watts, R. (2014). Reducing Risk for Youth by Promoting Healthy Development with Pyramid Mentoring: A Proposal for a Culturally Centered Group Mentoring. *Journal of Human Behavior in the Social Environment*, Vol. 24, pp.646-657.

Watson, J., Washington, G., & Stepteau-Watson, D. (2015). Umoja: A Culturally Specific Approach to Mentoring Young African-American Males. *Child Adolescence Social Work*, Vol. 32, pp. 81-90.

Weiler, L., Zarich, K., Haddock, S., Krafchick, J., and Zimmerman, T. (2014). A Comprehensive Model of Mentor Experiences: Perceptions, Strategies and Outcomes. *Journal of Community Psychology*, Vol. 42, No. 5, pp.593-608.

Whitaker, I. P., Whitaker, M. M., & Jackson, K. (2014). Single-parenting in the African-American Community: Implications for Public Policy and Practice. *Journal of Human Behavior in the Social Science*, Vol. 24, pp.230-249.

Wood, P., & Leck, J. (2008). Dysfunctional Mentoring. *The International Journal of Diversity in Organizations, Communities and Nations*, Vol. 8, No. 4.

Zastrow, C., & Kirst-Ashman, K. K. (2001). Psychological Systems and their Impacts on Middle Adulthood. In [Authored book] Understanding Human Behavior and the Social Environment (5th ed.), (pp.426-472). Belmont, California: Wadsworth.

Appendix A
Youth Participant Interview Questions

1) Tell me about yourself as it relates to your upbringing?
2) How do you see the community in which you currently live?
3) What is mentoring?
4) What has been your previous experience with mentoring programs?
5) Please share when you were first introduced to mentoring and how did you feel about having a mentor?
6) How long have you been coming to the Community Youth Center?
7) Why do you come to the Community Youth Center?
8) What programs or activities are you involved in at the Community Youth Center?
9) What do you consider a good mentor-mentee relationship?
10) What do you consider a bad mentor-mentee relationship?
11) Do you have a preference of whom you would like to be your mentor? For example, do they need to be the same race, ethnicity or gender?
12) How do you like the Extend-a-Hand Program?
13) When you hear the term "at-risk" what immediately comes to your mind and how does it make you feel?
14) What are your short-term goals and how do you plan to achieve them over the next year?

15) What are your long-term goals and how do you plan to achieve them over the next 2-5 years?

16) How do you value mentor relationships?

17) How are mentor relationships different or similar to the relationships you have with family members like parents, siblings, cousins, etc.?

18) If you had a good relationship with your mentor how likely would you share some of your innermost thoughts and feelings?

19) How likely do you believe your mentor can relate to your upbringing and be effective in understanding your circumstances or what you are going through?

20) How safe is the neighborhood where the Community Youth Center is located?

21) Do you believe the Community Youth Center helps to reduce crime, violence and dangerous activity in the community?

22) How comfortable would you be to invite your mentor to your home and how comfortable would you be to visit his/her home?

23) What is the most positive experience you have had with your mentor and what is the most disappointing?

24) Do you believe your mentor has the capacity to help you escape the realities of your circumstances?

25) What person has inspired you the most and why? (Your response can be family, friends, or people you have never formally met.)

Appendix B
Youth Participant Profiles

Name	Age	Grade	Reason for Referral
Jalen	14	Freshman	Extremely Low-income
Justin	14	Freshman	Extremely Low-income
Marion	17	Junior	Poor Academics, Behavior and Family Dysfunction
Marshauna	13	8th grade	Family Dysfunction
Shaundrel	18	Senior	Poor Academics
Marcus	17	Junior	Criminal Infraction
Terrell	15	Freshman	Criminal Infraction
Cortez	16	Sophomore	Family Dysfunction and Behavior
Jason	15	Freshman	Criminal Infraction
Destiny	14	8th grade	Family Dysfunction

Appendix C

Staff Participant Interview Questions

1) What are your name, title and current role at the Community Youth Center?

2) What is your educational background?

3) What made you decide to join the Community Youth Center?

4) What are your goals for the members you serve?

5) What is your definition of mentoring?

6) What is your definition of at-risk?

7) What are the biggest challenge and greatest reward of working with members of the Community Youth Center?

8) What are the primary issues or circumstances members face and how do you help address those issues?

9) Explain the Extend-a-Hand Program and its structure?

10) Explain how mentors are selected for the Extend-a-Hand Program and do they have any formal training prior to meeting with their mentees?

11) How do you develop and/or oversee programs and how do you measure their success?

12) Have you been a mentor or mentee and if so explain your experience?

About the Publisher

LIFE TO LEGACY LLC

Let us bring your story to life! Life to Legacy offers the following publishing services: manuscript development, editing, transcription services, ghost writing, cover design, copyright services, ISBN assignment, worldwide distribution, and eBooks.

Throughout the entire production process, you maintain control over your project. Even if you have no manuscript, we can ghost-write your story for you from audio recordings or legible handwritten documents. Whether print-on-demand or trade publishing, we have publishing packages to meet your needs. We make the production and publishing processes easy.

We also specialize in family history books, so you can leave a written legacy for your children, grandchildren, and others. You put your story in our hands, and we'll bring it to literary life!

Please visit our website:
www.Life2Legacy.com

Or call us at:
877-267-7477

You can also email us at:
Life2Legacybooks@att.net

www.ingramcontent.com/pod-product-compliance
Lightning Source LLC
Chambersburg PA
CBHW031629160426
43196CB00006B/347